MÜNCHEN, 23. MAI 2015. Die meisterliche Spielwiese präsentiert sich nicht mehr im satten Grün. Eine Konfettikanone hat aus dem Rasen einen Teppich in den Bayern-Farben Rot und Weiß geblasen und eine festliche Stimmung in die Allianz Arena gezaubert.

MUNICH, MAY 23, 2015. The playing field no longer presents itself in a lush green. A confetti cannon transformed the pitch into a champions' carpet in Bayern's red and white and conjured a festive ambience in the Allianz Arena.

MÜNCHEN, 28. APRIL 2015. Der Punkt der Wahrheit. Von hier wurden unzählige Elfmeter verwandelt und Spiele entschieden. Unvergessen sind aber auch zwei Entscheidungen mit unglücklichem Ausgang. Das »Finale dahoam« gegen Chelsea und das deutsche Pokal-Halbfinale 2015 gegen Dortmund gingen nach Elfmeterschießen in der Allianz Arena verloren.

MUNICH, APRIL 28, 2015. A point of contention. From this spot, countless penalties have been taken and crucial matches decided. There have been memorable triumphs as well as some unforgettable defeats: The “final dahoam” and the 2015 German cup semi-final versus Dortmund were lost on penalties in the Allianz Arena.

MÜNCHEN, 14. APRIL 2009. Die neue Heimat des FC Bayern ist längt ein Wahrzeichen Münchens geworden. Die Arena fasst 75.000 Zuschauer inklusive 2.200 Business Seats und 106 Logen. Die spektakuläre Außenfassade aus Folienkissen wird bei den Heimspielen von 380.000 LED-Leuchten in rotes Licht getaucht.

MUNICH, APRIL 14, 2009. FC Bayern's new home has long since been a landmark in Northern Munich. The Arena has a capacity of 75,000, including 106 luxury boxes and 2,500 business seats. The spectacular exterior façade is made of foil panels and for Bayern's home games is ablaze in red, lit by 380,000 LED lamps.

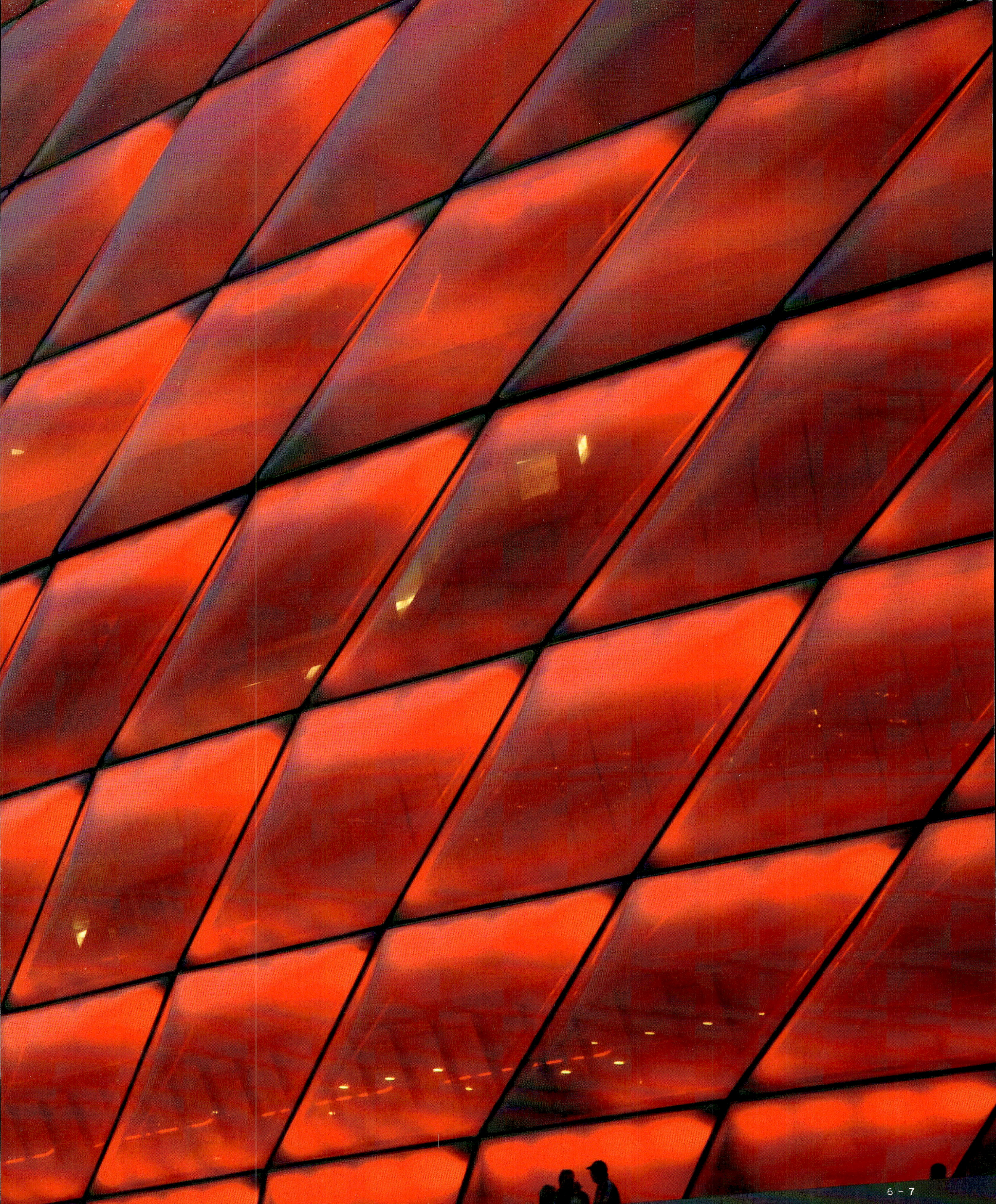

MÜNCHEN, 30. MAI 1973. Die erfolgreichste Achse der Vereinsgeschichte: Gerd Müller, Sepp Maier und Franz Beckenbauer stiegen gemeinsam in die Bundesliga auf, holten die erste Bundesliga-Meisterschaft, gewannen das erste Double, wurden Welt- und Europameister und siegten dreimal in Serie im Europapokal der Landesmeister.

MUNICH, MAY 30, 1973. The most prolific threesome in club history, Gerd Müller, Sepp Maier and Franz Beckenbauer. Together they won promotion to the Bundesliga, the club's first Bundesliga title and first domestic double, a World and European Championship as well as three consecutive European Cups.

Sepp Maier

MÜNCHEN, 21. SEPTEMBER 2015. Drei Pokale blitzen im Scheinwerferlicht. Ein Hattrick gelang den Bayern 1974, 75 und 76. Dreimal in Serie holten sie den Europapokal der Landesmeister und legten damit den Grundstein für ihre erfolgreiche Vereinsgeschichte. In der seit 1992/93 ausgetragenen Champions League konnte bisher kein Klub seinen Titel verteidigen.

MUNICH, SEPTEMBER 21, 2015. Sparkling silverware. Bayern achieved a European Cup hattrick in the seventies, winning the competition in 1974, 1975 and 1976, a feat that is the cornerstone of Bayern's international standing. Since the introduction of the UEFA Champions League in 1992, no team has managed to successfully defend its title.

MÜNCHEN, 11. MAI 2013. Die Legenden gratulieren dem Triple-Kapitän: Von Gerd Müller (vorne links) und Franz Beckenbauer (rechts) über Sepp Maier und Søren Lerby bis zu Oliver Kahn und Paulo Sergio klatschen die ehemaligen Stars Philipp Lahm ab. Bayern pflegt die Traditionen.

MUNICH, MAY 11, 2011. The captain of the treble-winning team among a host of legends. From Gerd Müller (front left) and Franz Beckenbauer (right) to Sepp Maier and Søren Lerby to Oliver Kahn and Paulo Sergio, the former stars all want to congratulate Philipp Lahm. Bayern honours its traditions.

BAYERN MÜNCHEN
21
LAHM

MÜNCHEN, 31. AUGUST 2014. Bayern pflegt die Tradition, der FC Bayern auch. Im Bayerischen Trachtenverband sind 180.000 Mitglieder vereint. Beim FC Bayern muss jeder Spieler beim traditionellen Oktoberfestbesuch in Tracht auflaufen. Dann stecken die Fußballerkörper in karierten Hemden, Lederhosen, Kniebundstrümpfen und Haferlschuhen.

MUNICH, AUGUST 31, 2014. Bavaria honours its traditions and so does FC Bayern. The Bayerischer Trachtenverband, the Bavarian Livery Association, has 180,000 members. The Bayern players don their Tracht for the traditional visit to the Oktoberfest and parade their athletic bodies in checkered shirts, Lederhosen, knee breeches and Haferl shoes.

LONDON, 25. MAI 2013. Die Schlacht ist geschlagen, das Spiel gewonnen. Zu sehen ist hier die Kabine im Londoner Wembleystadion nach dem 2:1 gegen Dortmund, aufgehübscht mit Bayern-Logo und dem Schriftzug des Finales der UEFA Champions League.

LONDON, MAY 25, 2013. The battle is fought, the game won. The dressing room in London's Wembley Stadium after the 2-1 win over Dortmund, adorned with Bayern's crest and the UEFA Champions League Final's logo.

WIEN, 3. AUGUST 1971. Das Foto von Franz Beckenbauer neben der Büste des österreichischen Kaisers Franz Joseph I. zeigt die Szene, mit der es zu seinem legendären Spitznamen gekommen ist. Geschossen wurde es von dem Wiener Fotografen Herbert Sündhofer anlässlich eines Freundschaftsspiels der Bayern anno 1971 in Wien. Der österreichische Journalist Sepp Graf komponierte dazu den Text vom »Fußball-Kaiser« – der Rest ist Geschichte.

VIENNA, AUGUST 3, 1971. It was this photo of him standing beside a bust of Austrian Emperor (Kaiser) Franz Joseph I. that Franz Beckenbauer owed his famous nickname to. The picture was taken by Viennese photographer Herbert Sündhofer while Bayern paid a visit to the Austrian capital for a friendly match in 1971. Austrian journalist Sepp Graf added an article about the "Fußball-Kaiser" – and the rest is history.

MÜNCHEN, 23. MÄRZ 2002. Manche tragen ihr Herz auf der Zunge, andere ihre Leidenschaft im Gesicht. Diese drei Schönheiten haben als Make-up das Bayern-Logo aufgetragen und dokumentieren so, was ihre Herzenssache ist. Fans sind zweifellos erfinderisch.

MUNICH, MARCH 23, 2002. Some wear their hearts on their sleeves, others their passion on their faces. These three beauties painted theirs with the club's logo to show their true colours. Fans are ingenious.

YER
FC BAYE
MÜNCH

ROM, 22. OKTOBER 2014, VATIKAN. Die Unterschriften auf dem Spielball wirken wie ein schriftliches Versprechen an den Papst. Bei einer Privataudienz im Vatikan sicherten die Bayern dem Heiligen Vater Einnahmen aus einem Freundschaftsspiel für karikative Zwecke zu und übergaben später einen Scheck über eine Million Euro für notleidende Menschen.

ROME, OCTOBER 22, 2014, VATICAN. The signatures on the ball serve as a promise to the Pope: at a private audience at the Vatican, Bayern pledged to donate all proceeds of a friendly match to charitable causes and later presented Francis with a cheque for one million Euros to aid people in need.

MÜNCHEN, FRÜHJAHR 2015. Das Bayern-Areal von oben. Hinter der Front an der Säbener Straße versteckt sich das Trainingsareal des FC Bayern. Eingebettet in ein Wohngebiet liegen da fünf Rasen- und zwei Kunstrasenplätze, die nicht nur von den Profis genutzt werden. Mittendrin, gesäumt von sechs Bäumen, ist ein kleiner Biergarten versteckt. Nicht nur vom Präsidentenzimmer aus lässt sich so der Trainingsbetrieb verfolgen.

MUNICH, SPRING, 2015. The Bayern grounds from above. Behind the headquarters in the Säbener Strasse the Bayern training ground is hidden: seven pitches, five natural grass and two artificial turf, embedded in a residential area. In the middle of it, lined by six trees, is a small beer garden. So you don't need to reside in the presidential office to get a good look at practice.

MÜNCHEN, 12. MAI 2015. Der Künstler bei der Arbeit, durch die Linse des Fotografen ganz nah herangerückt: Xabi Alonso, hier beim Eckball, kam als zweifacher Gewinner der Champions League nach München. Mit Real Madrid und dem FC Liverpool hat er bereits Europas Krone gewonnen.

MUNICH, MAY 12, 2015. The artist at work, as seen through the photographer's lens: Xabi Alonso, captured taking a corner, came as a two-time Champions League winner to Munich. He has been at the top of European football with Real Madrid and Liverpool.

MÜNCHEN, 19. MAI 2012. Bastian Schweinsteiger schlägt die Hände vor sein Gesicht. Er hat seinen Elfmeter an den Pfosten gesetzt, was Chelsea London wenig später zum Champions-League-Sieger macht. Ein Bild mit Symbolcharakter für das verlorene »Finale dahoam«.

MUNICH, MAY 19, 2012. Bastian Schweinsteiger buries his face in his hands: he missed the decisive penalty, hitting the post and thus making Chelsea Champions League champions. An image that came to symbolise the lost "final dahoam".

10
HUMMELS
15
4
PISZCZEK
26

LONDON, 25. MAI 2013. Das Tor der Entscheidung: Wie Slalomstangen hat Arjen Robben die Dortmunder Abwehrspieler umtanzt und lässt auch Torwart Weidenfeller keine Chance. Es ist der 2:1-Siegtreffer in der 89. Minute im ersten rein deutschen Endspiel in der Champions League.

LONDON, MAY 25, 2013. The deciding goal: Arjen Robben slaloms around Dortmund's defence and beats a helpless Roman Weidenfeller to make it 2-1 in the 89th minute, the winning goal in the competition's first ever all-German final.

adidas
MAGIRUS DEUTZ
BAYERN MÜNCHEN
5

MÜNCHEN, 23. NOVEMBER 2014. Zeugnisse der Bayern-Historie glänzen in einer Vitrine in der »Erlebniswelt«, dem Museum in der Allianz Arena. Die Trikots erzählen von einzelnen Epochen, großen Triumphen und der Treue von Werbepartnern und sind ein begehrtes Fotomotiv.

MUNICH, NOVEMBER 23, 2014. Bayern's history is showcased in the "Erlebniswelt", the museum in the Allianz Arena. The shirts bear witness to different eras, great triumph and loyal sponsors. And, naturally, they are also popular subjects for photographs.

MÜNCHEN, 21. APRIL 2010. Aufmarsch zum Angriff auf das Finale. Bayern trifft in der Champions League auf Olympique Lyon. Die Fans haben ein gutes Gespür für die Herausforderung und charakterisieren das Halbfinalhinspiel mit zwei Worten: »Pack ma's«. Sie packten es. Auf das 1:0 in München folgte ein 3:0 in Lyon.

MUNICH, APRIL 21, 2010. Run-up to the run on the final: Bayern faces Olympique Lyon. The fans have a good feel for the match and come up with a fitting motto for the first leg of the semi-final: "Pack ma's" (let's do it). They did it, winning 1-0 in Munich and wrapping it up with a convincing 3-0 in Lyon.

UniCredit
MasterCard
Maestro
SONY BRAVIA

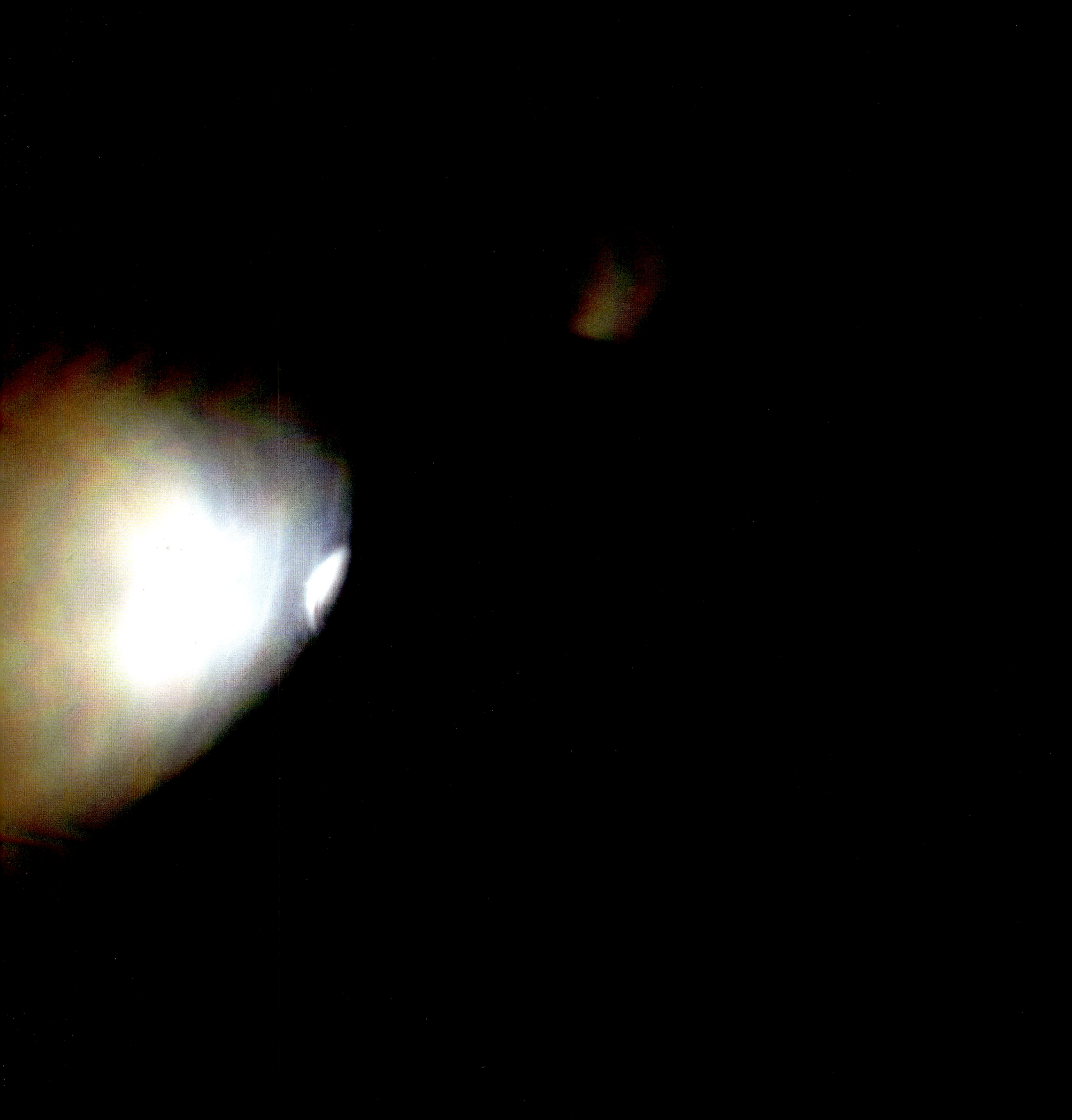

MOSKAU, 29. SEPTEMBER 2014. Ausländische Trainer haben dem FC Bayern stets neue Impulse gegeben. Mit Pep Guardiola übernahm der wohl begehrteste Trainer der Welt im Jahr 2013 die Triple-Sieger. Der Spanier hatte mit dem FC Barcelona zuvor in vier Jahren 14 Titel gewonnen. Dass er sich für München entschied, sprach auch für den internationalen Stellenwert des FC Bayern und des deutschen Fußballs.

MOSCOW, SEPTEMBER 29, 2014. Foreign coaches have always had a huge impact on FC Bayern. In 2013, the reigning treble winners successfully landed the services of probably the most coveted manager on the planet in Pep Guardiola. In four years at Barcelona, the Spaniard had won 14 titles and had his pick of pretty much every top club in Europe. The fact that he chose Bayern speaks to the club's and German football's international standing.

MÜNCHEN, 2015. Die Schatzkiste des FC Bayern ist in der »Erlebniswelt« ausgestellt. Kapitän Conny Heitkamp hatte die ersten Bayern-Pokale in den Wirren des Zweiten Weltkriegs bei einem Landwirt vergraben und so die Trophäen für den Verein bewahrt.

MUNICH, 2015. FC Bayern's treasure chest displayed in the "Erlebniswelt". Skipper Conny Heitkamp buried the first trophies on a farm during the Second World War, thus ensuring the silverware stayed with the club.

INHALT
CONTENTS

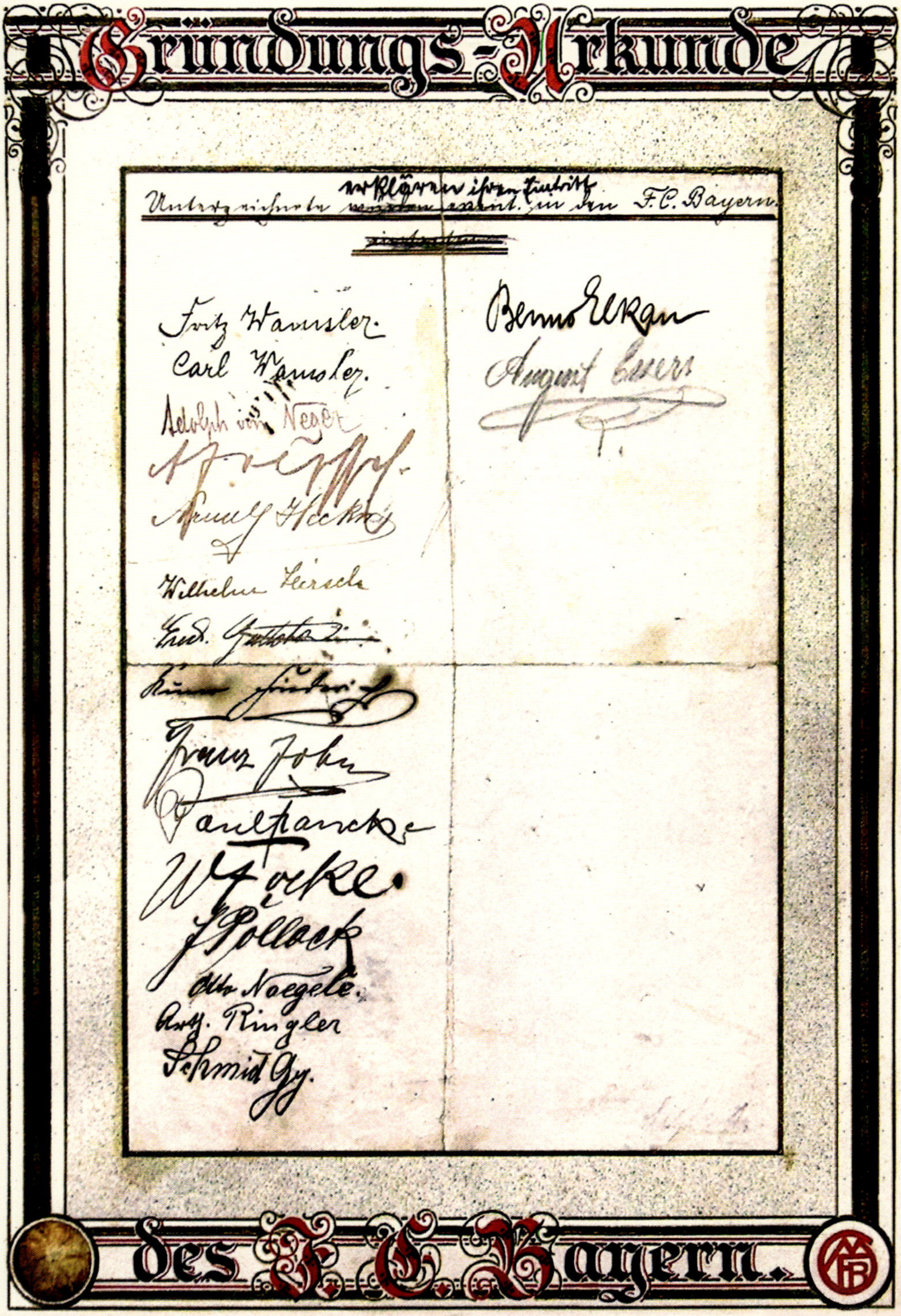

Gründungs-Urkunde

Unterzeichnete erklären ihren Eintritt in den F.C. Bayern.

Fritz Wamsler

Carl Wamsler

Adolph von Neyer

Wilhelm

Franz John

Paul Francke

W. Focke

J. Pollack

Otto Naegele

Rud. Ringler

Schmid Gg.

Benno Elkan

August

des F. C. Bayern.

MÜNCHEN, 27. FEBRUAR 1900. Die Gründungsurkunde des FC Bayern München.
MUNICH, FEBRUARY 27, 1900. The founding charter of FC Bayern München.

Liebe Leserinnen und Leser,
liebe Fußball-Freunde,

als ich mit 18 Jahren aus Lippstadt zum FC Bayern kam, war der Verein Europa- und Weltpokalsieger. Fast 40 Jahre später haben wir die Trophäensammlung ausgebaut und national wie international eine Spitzenstellung eingenommen.
Erfolg ist die Basis aller großen Klubs. Aber ein Klub wie der FC Bayern wird nur dann zum Mythos, wenn zu den legendären Siegen auch legendäre Niederlagen kommen. Wenn es Dramen gibt, wenn Tränen fließen und wir lernen, Enttäuschungen zu akzeptieren, um gestärkt nächste Ziele ins Auge zu nehmen.
Der FC Bayern hat aus seiner Geschichte eine Philosophie entwickelt, an der wir uns orientieren und die uns immer wieder neu motiviert und auch verpflichtet.
Was den FC Bayern ausmacht, dokumentiert dieses Buch in eindrucksvollen Fotos.
Viel Spaß wünscht

Karl-Heinz Rummenigge
VORSTANDSVORSITZENDER FC BAYERN MÜNCHEN AG

Dear readers,
dear football friends,

When I joined FC Bayern from Lippstadt as an 18-year-old, the club was the reigning European Cup and Club World Cup champion. Now, nearly 40 years later, we have won many more trophies and earned a place among the top clubs, nationally as well as internationally.
Success is the foundation of all big clubs. But a club like FC Bayern only becomes a legend when the legendary wins are joined by equally legendary defeats. When there are dramas, when tears are flowing, and when we learn to accept the disappointments and set about achieving our goals with new vigour.
From its history Bayern developed a philosophy that provides us with orientation and that serves as motivation as well as obligation.
In impressive photos, this book documents all that defines FC Bayern.
Enjoy!

Karl-Heinz Rummenigge
CHIEF EXECUTIVE OFFICER, FC BAYERN MÜNCHEN AG

»Das Wichtigste beim FC Bayern ist der Erfolg. Aber wir dürfen auch andere Aspekte nicht vergessen: Fair Play zum Beispiel, auch in Niederlagen Größe zu zeigen. Das hat der FC Bayern immer wieder gezeigt.«
PHILIPP LAHM

"The most important thing at FC Bayern is success. But we must not overlook other aspects: fair play, for example, being graceful in defeat. Those are traits that FC Bayern has always honoured."
PHILIPP LAHM

Es sind die unvergessenen Spiele, die sich einprägen und den Mythos begründen. Dazu gehören große Siege genauso wie dramatische Niederlagen. Sie haben den FC Bayern nur stärker gemacht.

It's the unforgettable games that are forever etched in collective memory and create a legend. They include great triumphs as well as dramatic defeats. But throughout their history, they only served to make Bayern stronger.

MÜNCHEN, 16. JULI 2015. Für die Deutsche Meisterschaft gibt es keinen Pokal, sondern die Meisterschale. Bereits seit 1987 ist Bayern Deutschlands Rekordmeister, bis zum Jahr 2015 wird der Name FC Bayern München 25-mal in die Schale eingraviert. In den Kölner Werkschulen geschmiedet, wird sie seit 1949 dem jeweiligen Meister übergeben.

MUNICH, JULY 16, 2015. The winners of the Bundesliga do not receive a cup, but the "Meisterschale". Bayern have been Germany's record champions since 1987 and by now have etched their name into the trophy 25 times. The "Meisterschale", forged in the Kölner Werkschulen, has been presented to the respective champion since 1949.

1985 FC BAYERN MÜNCHE
2000 FC BAYERN MÜNCHEN
2015 FC BAYERN MÜNCHEN
BERLIN · 1906 VFB.
NÜRNBERG/HSV ·
BERLIN · 1932

LIVERPOOL, 8. APRIL 1981. Walter Junghans, als Nachfolger des 1979 verunglückten Sepp Maier die Nummer eins im Bayern-Tor, hatte seine größte Nervenprobe im Halbfinale des Europapokals der Landesmeister an der legendären Anfield Road zu bestehen. Die berühmte Tribüne »The Kop« mit den Liverpooler Fans, wo die Hymne »You'll Never Walk Alone« angestimmt wird, reicht bis ans Spielfeld, bis an den Torhüter heran. Junghans hält in diesem Match die Null, gewinnt das Nervenspiel.

LIVERPOOL, APRIL 8, 1981. Don't Look Now. He may not see them, but Walter Junghans can surely hear the home fans that fill the famous "Kop" at Liverpool's Anfield Road, where the tradition of singing "You'll Never Walk Alone" was born in the early sixties. Junghans had succeeded Sepp Maier in goal, after the former number one sustained serious injuries in a car crash in 1979. Junghans managed to keep a clean sheet in this match, the European Cup semifinal.

31
SCHWEINSTEIGER
FCB

MÜNCHEN, 19. MAI 2012. Die Augen von Ivica Olic starren ins Leere, Bastian Schweinsteiger vergräbt sein Gesicht im Rasen. Die Bayern am Boden, der Traum ist zerplatzt. Als erster Verein wollte der FCB den Titel im eigenen Stadion gewinnen. Aber das »Finale dahoam« (bayerisch für Finale zu Hause) gewann der FC Chelsea mit 4:3 im Elfmeterschießen und holte 2012 erstmals die Champions-League-Trophäe. Es wurde ein »Drama dahoam«.

MUNICH, MAY 19, 2012. Bastian Schweinsteiger buries his face in the grass and Ivica Olic gazes emptily into the distance. Bayern are defeated, their dream shattered. FCB hoped to become the first club to win the title in their own stadium. But the "final dahoam" (Bavarian for "final at home") turned to heartbreak dahoam: Chelsea won 4-3 on penalties and clinched their first ever Champions League title.

MÜNCHEN, 2. NOVEMBER 1983. UEFA-Cup 1983/84, zweite Runde, das Rückspiel. Nach 18 Elfmetern steht der Sieger zwischen Bayern und PAOK Saloniki noch immer nicht fest. Jean-Marie Pfaff, der Belgier im Bayern-Tor, hat zuvor einen Strafstoß pariert, läuft nun selbst an und zimmert den Ball in den Torwinkel. Saloniki mit Trainer Pal Csernai ist nach einem dramatischen Shoot-out ausgeschieden.

MUNICH, NOVEMBER 2, 1983. UEFA Cup 1983–84, second round, return leg. After nine rounds of penalties, the match between Bayern and PAOK Saloniki still isn't settled. The Belgian goalkeeper Jean-Marie Pfaff has saved PAOK's latest attempt and now has a chance to put his team through. He makes his run and hammers the ball into the corner. Saloniki with coach Pal Csernai bow out after a dramatic shoot-out.

FC BAYERN -
PAOK SALONIKI
8 : 8

nfaser

MÜNCHEN, 23. APRIL 1994. Wir sehen Thomas Helmer und Nürnbergs Torwart Andreas Köpke. Wir sehen den Ball, der neben das Tor trudeln wird. An jenem 32. Spieltag der Saison 1993/94 erkannte Schiedsrichter Osmers das Tor an, das keines war. Dieses Phantomtor entschied Meisterschaft und Abstieg. Erstmals widerrief der DFB eine Tatsachenentscheidung des Schiedsrichters, ließ die Partie wiederholen. Bayern siegte 5:0 statt 2:1, wurde Meister. Nürnberg stieg ab.

MUNICH, APRIL 23, 1994. It's the 32nd match day of the season 1993-94. Thomas Helmer is standing over Nuremberg's prone keeper Andreas Köpke, the ball trundles over the goal line, going wide for all to see. Except for referee Osmers, who awards a goal. The DFB, however, decides to annul the result and order a replay. It marks the first time ever the association overrules an official's factual decision. The rematch proves to be crucial for both clubs: Bayern wins 5-0 and clinches the Bundesliga title, Nuremberg gets relegated due to an inferior goal difference.

BERLIN, 26. JUNI 1965. Bundesliga, wir kommen! Um 17.42 Uhr kannte der Jubel im Berliner Olympiastadion keine Grenzen mehr: Der 8:0-Sieg bei Tennis Borussia durch Tore von Ohlhauser (4), Nafziger (2), Müller und Brenninger machte den Bundesliga-Aufstieg endlich perfekt. Die Fans schultern Brenninger und den neuen Torjäger Gerd Müller.

BERLIN, JUNE 26, 1965. Bundesliga, here we come! After narrowly missing out the year before, Bayern were hoping to finally win promotion to the Bundesliga in 1965. At 5.42 pm on June 26 they had finally done it in the Olympic Stadium of Berlin - and they did so in convincing fashion, disposing of Tennis Borussia an 8-0 trouncing on goals by Ohlhauser (4), Nafziger (2), Müller and Brenninger.

FRANKFURT, 1. MAI 1982. So werden Helden geboren. Das Pokalfinale 1982 trägt einen Namen: Dieter Hoeneß, der Mann mit dem Turban. Nach einem Kopfballduell mit dem Nürnberger Alois Reinhardt (15.) hatte er sich eine Risswunde an der Stirn zugezogen. Immer wieder musste die blutdurchtränkte Kopfbandage gewechselt werden. Auch dank seines vorbildlichen Einsatzes drehten die Bayern ein 0:2. Den Schlusspunkt zum 4:2 setzte Hoeneß selbst – mit einem Kopfballtor. Der Turban wird zum Sinnbild bayerischen Siegeswillens.

FRANKFURT, MAY 1, 1982. The 1982 German cup final will foreve- be associated with one name: Dieter Hoeneß, the man in the turban. After a clash with Nuremberg's Alois Reinhardt (15.) he suffered a bad cut on the forehead. The blood-soaked bandages had to be changed over and over. But thanks to his determination and perseverance Bayern turned the match after trailing 0-2. On 89 minutes he headed home Breitner's cross to make it a 4-2 final. The turban came tc symbolise the Bavarian will to win.

NÜRNBERG, 31. MAI 1967. Der erste internationale Titel. Im Europapokalfinale der Pokalsieger 1967 siegen die Bayern durch ein Tor von Franz »Bulle« Roth mit 1:0 (108. Minute) gegen die Glasgow Rangers. Es ist ihr erster internationaler Titel. Roth zeigte hier zum ersten Mal, dass in Spielen um wichtige Titel besonders mit ihm zu rechnen war. Er traf noch zwei weitere Male in einem europäischen Cupfinale. Nach seinem ersten Erfolg nahm er den Pokal mit auf sein Hotelzimmer.

NUREMBERG, MAY 31, 1967. The young Bayern team beat the odds to reach the 1967 Cup Winners' Cup final, which almost turned into a home game. Their opponents this time were Glasgow Rangers, Bayern won on a goal by Franz "Bulle" Roth in the 108th minute: their first international triumph. Roth gained a reputation for coming up big in crucial moments, scoring in two other European Cup Finals. He obviously loved silverware, as evidenced in the photo.

BREMEN, 22. APRIL 1986. Dieser Elfmeter entschied die Meisterschaft 1986. Am 33. Spieltag kam es zum direkten Duell zwischen Bremen und Bayern. Ein Sieg hätte Werder den Titel gesichert. 0:0 stand es bis zur 88. Minute, dann entschied Schiedsrichter Volker Roth auf Handelfmeter. Michael Kutzop hatte zuvor 39 Strafstöße in der Bundesliga verwandelt und nie verschossen. Jetzt lief er an, tanzte Jean-Marie Pfaff aus – traf aber nur den rechten Pfosten. Bayern nutzte die unverhoffte Chance, gewann am letzten Spieltag 6:0 gegen Gladbach, während Bremen in Stuttgart 1:2 verlor. Udo Lattek triumphierte über Otto Rehhagel, weil Kutzops Elfmeter am Pfosten hängen blieb …

BREMEN, APRIL 22, 1986. The penalty that decided the 1986 Bundesliga title race. When Bayern travelled to Bremen on match day 33, their hosts needed a win to clinch the championship. With the game still scoreless after 88 minutes, referee Volker Roth awarded Werder a penalty. Michael Kutzop had converted 39 penalties in the Bundesliga and never missed. He had Jean-Marie Pfaff going the wrong way, but hit the post. Bayern seized the unexpected opportunity and beat Gladbach 6–0 in their final game of the season, while Bremen lost 1–2 in Stuttgart. Udo Lattek prevailed over Otto Rehhagel, all because Kutzop's penalty struck the post.

MÜNCHEN, 24. OKTOBER 1973. Das erste Duell Ost gegen West. Es wurde zum sportlichen Klassenkampf stilisiert. Erstmals hatte das Europacup-Los zwei deutsche Mannschaften gegeneinander geführt. BRD-Meister FC Bayern gegen DDR-Meister Dynamo Dresden. In München lag Dynamo bei Halbzeit mit 3:2 vorn, Franz Roth und Gerd Müller drehten die Partie zum 4:3-Sieg. Das Rückspiel in Dresden am 7. November wurde zum Politikum. Ganz Fußball-Deutschland West atmete nach dem 3:3 auf, der Klassenkampf war gewonnen. Es war das vielleicht erste Mal, dass sich eine große Mehrheit der Fußballfans im Westen mit den Münchnern solidarisierte.

MUNICH, OCTOBER 24, 1973. The first duel East vs. West. It was stylised as a footballing class struggle. The clash between West German champions Bayern and East German champions Dynamo Dresden marked the first time that teams from both German states were pitted against each other in a European Cup competition. Both teams fought tooth and nail. Dresden led 3-2 at half-time in Munich, Bayern rallied on goals by Franz Roth and Gerd Müller to win 4-3. The second leg on November 7 in Dresden was fraught with political implications. The whole football community in West Germany rejoiced, the class struggle after the 3:3 was won. It may have been the first time that a vast majority of fans in the West sided with the team from Munich.

MAILAND, 23. MAI 2001. 25 Jahre war es her. Seit 1976 waren alle Versuche gescheitert, den Henkelpott wieder nach München zu holen. 1982, 1987 und 1999 hatte es bittere Finalniederlagen gegeben. Aber die Mannschaft von Ottmar Hitzfeld zeigte zwei Jahre nach dem unglücklichen Ausgang des Endspiels gegen Manchester United Charakter und erreichte das Ziel: Sie gewann die Champions League durch ein 6:5 nach dem Elfmeterschießen gegen den FC Valencia, wobei Oliver Kahn gleich drei Versuche der gegnerischen Schützen parierte.

MILAN, MAY 23, 2001. It had been 25 years. Since 1976, any and all attempts to bring the trophy back to Munich came up short. They had suffered heartbreaking finals losses in 1982, 1987 und 1999. But wo years after the last-minute shock against Manchester United, Ottmar Hitzfeld's team showed their mettle and got the job done: they won the Champions League, beating Valencia 6-5 after the penalty shoot-out. Oliver Kahn saved three attempts.

MÜNCHEN, 7. MÄRZ 1970. Derbys, we miss you. Als die Bundesliga gegründet wurde, erhielt nur ein Münchner Klub die Startgenehmigung: der TSV 1860. Die offiziellen Münchner Geschichtsschreiber haben bis 2015 insgesamt 204 Lokalderbys registriert. Mit 105 Siegen und nur 49 Niederlagen spricht die Bilanz eindeutig für den FC Bayern. Trotzdem bedauern selbst Bayern-Fans die fehlenden Derbys und ihre Brisanz. Seit 2004 sind die »Löwen« nicht mehr erstklassig.

MUNICH, MARCH 7, 1970. Missing the Derby. When the Bundesliga was founded in 1963, only one club from Munich gained entry: TSV 1860. According to officially recorded history, by 2015 the teams had met in 204 derbies; Bayern won 105 of them and lost only 49. The "lions", however, have been absent from the Bundesliga since 2004 and Bayern and TSV fans alike dearly miss the derbies and their drama.

SPARKASSE

WIEN, 27. MAI 1987. Selten gab es einen deutlicheren Favoriten in einem Finale wie 1987. Bayern ging gegen Porto auch noch in Führung. »Wiggerl« Kögl traf zum 1:0 (25.). Aber die Münchner hatten die Rechnung ohne den Algerier Rabah Madjer gemacht. Mit der Hacke überwand er Jean-Marie Pfaff (78.) und legte zwei Minuten später das Siegtor für Juary auf. Die Hacke zerstörte den Bayern-Traum, elf Jahre nach dem letzten Triumph im Europapokal der Landesmeister den Pokal wieder nach München zu holen. Udo Lattek, der zuvor seinen Abschied von den Bayern verkündet hatte, blieb der große Erfolg zum Ausklang verwehrt.

VIENNA, MAY 27, 1987. Bayern were prohibitive favourites to win the 1987 European Cup Final in Vienna against the Portuguese underdogs from Porto. They duly took an early lead on "Wiggerl" Kögl's goal on 25 minutes. But they had not reckoned with Porto's striker Rabah Madjer. He artfully beat Jean-Marie Pfaff with a nifty back-heel goal and just two minutes later set up Juary for the winner. Madjer's back-heel destroyed Bayern's dream of bringing the trophy back to Munich after eleven years. Udo Lattek who had already announced his departure from Munich had to say goodbye without having won the much coveted trophy this time.

EOS

MÜNCHEN, 27. NOVEMBER 1971. Rekordsieg gegen den BVB. Im November 1971 kamen gerade 17.000 Zuschauer in das Stadion an der Grünwalder Straße. Sie erlebten am 16. Spieltag der Saison 1971/72 den höchsten Bundesliga-Sieg der Bayern. Das 11:1 durch Tore von Müller (4), Hoeneß, Roth (je 2), Hoffmann, Beckenbauer und Breitner blieb bis 2015 ihr einziger zweistelliger Sieg.

MUNICH, NOVEMBER 27, 1971. Biggest win vs BVB. Just 17,000 made the pilgrimage to the Grünwalder Strasse to see the clash on match day 16 of the 1971-72 season. They witnessed Bayern's biggest Bundesliga win: 11-1, on goals by Müller (4), Hoeneß, Roth (2 each), Hoffmann, Beckenbauer and Breitner. It remains their only win in double figures till 2015.

DORTMUND
1

adidas

BARCELONA, 26. MAI 1999. Der Blick geht ins Leere, die Trophäe bleibt unerreicht. Lothar Matthäus hat alles gewonnen, nur die Champions League nicht. In Barcelona war er so nahe dran wie nie. Aber Bayern verlor gegen Manchester United mit 1:2. Es war die »Mutter aller Niederlagen«. Denn Bayern führte 1:0, sah wie der sichere Sieger aus und verlor in der Nachspielzeit durch Tore von Sheringham und Solskjaer.

BARCELONA, MAY 26, 1999. Lothar Matthäus not even gazes at the elusive trophy. The midfielder had won everything, only the Champions League remained out of reach. In Barcelona he came painfully close, but Bayern was defeated by Manchester United. It was the "mother of all defeats", as Bayern took an early 1-0 lead and appeared well on their way to victory, before Sheringham and Solskjaer struck in injury time.

MÖNCHENGLADBACH, 26. FEBRUAR 1972. Günter Netzer und Franz Beckenbauer: große Rivalen und dicke Freunde. Beide Kapitäne prägten in den 1970er Jahren den deutschen Fußball, Bayern und Gladbach gewannen in diesem Jahrzehnt zusammen acht Meistertitel. Die Freundschaft hat die Rivalität überdauert.

MÖNCHENGLADBACH, FEBRUARY 26, 1972. Günter Netzer and Franz Beckenbauer: big rivals and even better friends. As the captains of their respective teams, both men shaped the German football of the 1970s. During this decade Bayern and Gladbach won eight championships between them. Beckenbauers's and Netzer's friendship outlasted the rivalry.

MÜNCHEN, 28. JUNI 1972. Die Konstellation war einmalig: Bayern führte in der Spielzeit 1971/72 die Tabelle mit einem Punkt Vorsprung vor Schalke 04 an, das zum letzten Saisonspiel nach München kam. Es gab also ein echtes Finale zur Eröffnung des Olympiastadions. 80.000 Zuschauer kamen, spülten die erste Millioneneinnahme in die Kasse. Bayern siegte beeindruckend mit 5:1. Bis 2005 feierte der FC Bayern unter dem berühmten Zeltdach 17 Deutsche Meisterschaften.

MUNICH, JUNE 28, 1972. The set-up was intriguing: in the 1971-72 season, Bayern were one point clear of visitors Schalke at the top of the standings, so it was a true final to open the new ground at the Olympiastadion. 80,000 filled the stadium, a nice windfall for Bayern's coffers. Bayern won in convincing fashion 5-1. Before moving to the Allianz Arena in 2005, they celebrated 17 league titles under the famous canopy.

BORDEAUX, 15. MAI 1996. Einst hatte Franz Beckenbauer den UEFA-Pokal-Wettbewerb als »Cup der Verlierer« bezeichnet. 1996 stand er selbst als Trainer im Finale, nachdem er Otto Rehhagel bei den Bayern auf diesem Posten abgelöst hatte. Und füllte die Vereinsvitrine mit einem weiteren Pokal. Denn erstmals gewann der FCB den UEFA-Cup. Stolz reckt Kapitän Matthäus die Trophäe in den französischen Nachthimmel.

BORDEAUX, MAY 15, 1996. Franz Beckenbauer once dubbed the UEFA Cup the "loser's Cup". Yet in 1996 he led Bayern to the final after taking the reins from Otto Rehhagel as head coach and added another trophy to Bayern's cabinet. It was their first triumph in the competition. Skipper Lothar Matthäus proudly raises the trophy into the French night sky.

BRÜSSEL, 15. MAI 1974. Ein Tor für die Geschichtsbücher. Im Finale des Landesmeisterpokals 1974 gegen Atlético Madrid lagen die Bayern 0:1 zurück – in allerletzter Sekunde fasste sich Hans-Georg »Katsche« Schwarzenbeck ein Herz und hämmerte den Ball aus 30 Metern zum 1:1 ins Netz. Daher musste das Spiel nach damaliger Regelung zwei Tage später wiederholt werden. Die Bayern gewannen durch Tore von Hoeneß (29./83.) und Müller (56./69.) mit 4:0. Erstmals hatte eine deutsche Elf den Pokal der Landesmeister geholt.

BRUSSELS, MAY 15, 1974. A goal for the history books. Bayern was trailing 0–1 in the European Cup final vs. Atlético Madrid. In the waning seconds, centre back Hans-Georg "Katsche" Schwarzenbeck stepped up and let it rip from 35 yards, finding the back of the net. Two days later the replay was held at the same venue and this time it was no contest: a dominating performance and braces by both Hoeneß (29./83.) and Müller (56./69.) made it 4–0 Bayern. It marked the first European Cup victory for a German side.

HAMBURG, 19. MAI 2001. Indirekter Freistoß für die Bayern in der 94. Minute. Die letzte Chance auf den Meistertitel. Nie zuvor hatte der Schwede Patrik Andersson für die Bayern getroffen. Jetzt schon. Durch unzählige Beine hindurch drosch er den Ball zum 1:1 gegen den Hamburger SV ins Netz. Ein Punktgewinn, der Bayern zum Titel reichte. Nur vier Minuten durfte Schalke vom Titel träumen.

HAMBURG, MAY 19, 2001. Indirect free kick for Bayern in the 94th minute. Their last chance to win the title. Swede Patrik Andersson had never scored a goal for Bayern before. But he does now. Through a maze of legs he hammers the ball, which finds its way into the back of the net and makes it 1-1 against Hamburger SV. Bayern earns a point, which is enough to secure the title. Schalke's championship dream lasted only four minutes.

14
FILA

D45

BRÜSSEL, 17. MAI 1974. Nie zuvor hatte eine deutsche Elf den Europapokal der Landesmeister gewonnen, der seit 1956 ausgespielt wird. 1974 begann eine neue Epoche. Entsprechend jubeln Sepp Maier, Uli Hoeneß, Hans-Georg Schwarzenbeck, Franz Roth und Johnny Hansen nach dem 4:0-Sieg im Wiederholungsspiel gegen Atlético Madrid. Es ist der Auftakt für den Titelhattrick der großen Bayern um Beckenbauer, Müller und Maier.

BRUSSELS, MAY 17, 1974. Never before had a German side won the European Cup, which had been contested since 1956. In 1974 a new era began. Here you see the ceremony of Sepp Maier, Uli Hoeneß, Hans-Georg Schwarzenbeck, Franz Roth und Johnny Hansen after the 4-0 victory against Atletico Madrid in the rematch. A legendary Bayern side with Beckenbauer, Müller and Maier has started and ends with the European Cup hattrick.

Red Wood Cats
LIPPACH
GAZPROM

MÜNCHEN, 23. APRIL 2013. Das Ergebnis klingt noch heute unfassbar. Bayern gegen Barcelona 7:0. Es war das Champions-League-Halbfinale 2013, als galaktische Bayern zuerst in München zauberten. Thomas Müller (25., 82.), Mario Gómez (49.) und Arjen Robben (73.) zermürbten Barça. Fußball in Perfektion, Kombinationswirbel, Tore der Extraklasse. Das Foto zeigt den Schlusspunkt von Thomas Müller, der auch im Rückspiel traf. Da siegten die Bayern durch Tore von Robben (49.), Piqué (ET, 72.) und Müller (76.) mit 3:0. Es waren zwei unvergessliche Galanächte.

MUNICH, APRIL 23, 2013. Even now the result still seems inconceivable. Bayern versus Barcelona: 7-0. It happened in the semi-final of the 2013 Champions League. Bayern put on an incredible show at home, defeating Barça 4-0 on goals by Thomas Müller (25., 82.), Mario Gómez (49.) and Arjen Robben (73.). Football in perfection, dazzling short passing and movement, wonderful goals. The photo shows Thomas Müller notching his second goal of the game. He would also score in the return leg, which ended 3-0 on two further goals by Robben (49.) and Piqué (o. g., 72.). Two gala performances for the ages.

TITEL FÜR DIE GESCHICHTSBÜCHER

TROPHIES FOR THE HISTORY BOOKS

Als die Bundesliga im August 1963 aus der Taufe gehoben wurde, fehlte der FC Bayern in der Startliste der 16 Teilnehmer. Die lapidare Begründung damals lautete: »Das Gremium war der Auffassung, dass es nicht ratsam erscheint, zwei Vereinen am gleichen Ort eine Lizenz für die Bundesliga zu erteilen.« Der TSV 1860 München, in der Oberliga einen Platz vor dem FC Bayern platziert, erhielt damals den Vorzug.

Längst aber ist der im Jahr 1900 gegründete FC Bayern Deutschlands Vorzeigeklub. Nach dem Aufstieg im Jahr 1965 mit den jungen bayerischen Talenten Maier, Müller und Beckenbauer bestieg der FC Bayern bereits 1987 Deutschlands Thron. Da gelang unter Trainer Udo Lattek der zehnte Meistertitel. Somit wurde der 1. FC Nürnberg mit neun Meisterschaften als Rekordmeister abgelöst. Die Dominanz in Deutschland ist seither unbestritten. Bis zum Jahr 2015 war die Titelsammlung auf 25 Meisterschaften und 17 Pokalsiege angewachsen. Dreimal gelang dabei der Titelhattrick (1972/73/74, 1985/86/87, 2013/14/15), zehnmal das Double und im Jahr 2013 sogar das Triple mit dem Gewinn von Meisterschaft, Pokal und Champions League.

Vor Beginn der Saison 2015/16 standen insgesamt 63 Titelgewinne in den Geschichtsbüchern. Und damit befindet sich der FC Bayern in einer Liga, in der nur noch Real Madrid und der FC Barcelona beheimatet sind. Während Manchester United oder Juventus Turin sogar die Tiefen der Zweitklassigkeit durchleben mussten, war der FC Bayern in den letzten 53 Jahren 49-mal für den europäischen Wettbewerb qualifiziert. Das zeigt seine Konstanz und nationale Dominanz über fünf Jahrzehnte. Zudem ist der FC Bayern neben Ajax Amsterdam, Juventus Turin und dem FC Chelsea einer von vier Klubs, die alle drei Europapokale gewonnen haben: 1967 den

When the Bundesliga was introduced in August 1963, FC Bayern was missing from the list of 16 teams that had gained entry. The rationale back then was: "The committee was of the opinion that it was not advisable to grant two clubs from the same locale permission for the Bundesliga." TSV 1860 München, who had finished ahead of Bayern in the previous Oberliga campaign, were chosen instead.

Since then, the club that was founded on February 27, 1900, has evolved into the premier football club in Germany. After winning promotion in 1965 with a squad of gifted young talents like Maier, Müller and Beckenbauer, Bayern soon established itself as a top club and in 1987, under coach Udo Lattek, permanently cemented their position at the top. That season Bayern won their tenth Bundesliga title, surpassing Nuremberg as record champions. Since then, their dominance has been unbroken. By now Bayern have won 25 German titles as well as 17 German cups. They won three consecutive championships on three occasions (1972–74, 1985–87, 2013–15), ten doubles, and in 2013 the unique treble of Bundesliga title, cup win and Champions League.

In all, the history books recorded 63 title wins prior to the 2015–16 season, placing Bayern in elite company with the likes of Real Madrid and FC Barcelona. While clubs like Manchester United and Juventus Turin even scaled the depths of the second division for a while, Bayern in the last 53 years qualified for a European competition a whopping 49 times, attesting to their consistency and domestic dominance over five decades.

Moreover, Bayern is one of only four clubs – Ajax Amsterdam, Juventus Turin and Chelsea being the others – that have won all three European cup competitions: the Cup Winners' Cup in 1967, the UEFA Cup in 1996 –

Europapokal der Pokalsieger, 1996 unter dem Trainer Franz Beckenbauer den UEFA-Pokal, den er selbst einmal als »Cup der Verlierer« bezeichnet hatte, dazu fünfmal den Europapokal der Landesmeister bzw. die Champions League. In der UEFA-Klub-Rangliste 2015 belegen die Münchner Platz drei hinter Real Madrid und dem FC Barcelona, sie gehörten von 2012 bis 2015 ununterbrochen zu den besten vier Klubs in der europäischen Königsklasse.

Zehnmal erreichten die Bayern das Finale im Europapokal der Landesmeister, der seit 1992/93 Champions League heißt. Große Siege waren darunter und bittere Niederlagen. 1987 gegen den FC Porto starteten die Münchner als großer Favorit, gingen durch Ludwig Kögl in Führung, kassierten das Hackentor des Algeriers Rabah Madjer und verloren schließlich mit 1:2. Unvergessen auch das Finale 1999 gegen Manchester United, in dem die Münchner bis zur 90. Minute durch einen Freistoßtreffer von Mario Basler in Führung lagen und dann den »Sekundentod« starben, als in der Nachspielzeit zunächst Teddy Sheringham der Ausgleich und Ole Gunnar Solskjaer sogar noch der Siegtreffer für ManU gelang. Da saßen die Bayern-Reservisten schon in den Champions-T-Shirts auf der Reservebank …

»Ohne diese bittere Niederlage hätten wir nicht die nächsten Titel geholt«, erinnert sich Oliver Kahn und verweist damit auf eine bajuwarische Stärke: den unbändigen Erfolgswillen. Im Jahr 2001, also nur zwei Jahre nach der bitteren Niederlage gegen ManU, holten die Bayern am 34. Spieltag durch ein 1:1 in der Nachspielzeit beim Hamburger SV eine weitere Deutsche Meisterschaft und gewannen nach 25 Jahren wieder den Königspokal im Elfmeterschießen gegen den FC Valencia.

Bayern-Gen wird dieser unbändige Siegeswille auch genannt. Unverbürgt ist das Gerücht, dass er jedem Spieler gleich mit der Vertragsunterschrift eingeimpft wird. Aber die Titelhamster von der Isar sind weiter unersättlich.

under coach Franz Beckenbauer, who famously once called it the "losers' cup" – and five times the European Cup/Champions League. In the 2015 UEFA club ranking, Bayern is third behind Real Madrid and FC Barcelona. From 2012 to 2015 they reached the final four of the Champions League in every season.

Bayern reached the final of the European Cup of Champions, which was renamed Champions League in 1993, ten times. They celebrated big triumphs but suffered also bitter defeats. In 1987 against Porto they were heavily favoured to win and duly took the lead on Ludwig Kögl's goal, before conceding Algerian Rabah Madjer's famous back-heel goal and eventually losing by 1–2. Deeply etched into Bayern's collective memory is the 1999 final in Barcelona, where they led on Basler's free-kick goal before they suffered a "sudden death", when both Teddy Sheringham and Ole Gunnar Solskjaer scored in injury time. Bayern's reserves on the bench at the time had already donned celebratory shirts.

"Without this bitter defeat, we would not have won the next title", Oliver Kahn remembers, referring to a Bavarian strength, their irrepressible will to win. In 2001, just two years after the defeat in Barcelona, Bayern secured another league title after scoring in injury time in Hamburg and then won the European Cup for the first time in 25 years after beating Valencia on penalties.

This absolute will to win is often referred to as the "Bayern gene". It is said that this trait is injected into a player's veins the moment he signs a contract with the team. So the next triumph is never far away.

»Wir haben aus dem verlorenen Finale 1999 gelernt, die Mentalität des Nie-Aufgebens in uns aufgesogen und in Willen entwickelt. So wurde 2001 belohnt, was die Grundessenz einer Bayern-Mannschaft sein muss: immer mit großem Selbstvertrauen aufzutreten.«
OLIVER KAHN

"We learned from our defeat in 1999, absorbed the never-say-die mentality and transformed it into an absolute will to win. Therefore 2001 was the reward for what has to be the essence of any Bayern team: to always perform with great confidence."
OLIVER KAHN

Was wäre der Fußball ohne Gefühle, auf dem Rasen und auf den Rängen? Jubelnde Fans mit herausragenden Choreografien, jubelnde Spieler nach großen Siegen und schönen Toren. Aber auch Wut, Enttäuschung und Willenskraft sind emotionale Regungen, die Schlagzeilen machen. Und manchmal fließen sogar Tränen…

Football would not be the same without its emotions, both on the pitch and in the stands. Cheering fans with their chants and choreographies, exultant players after big wins and beautiful goals. But the emotional range also encompasses frustration, fear, and anger… and sometimes these emotions even cause tears.

BERLIN, 17. MAI 2014. Freude pur. Der Brasilianer Dante reckt 2014 den DFB-Pokal nach einem 2:0-Sieg über Dortmund in den Berliner Nachthimmel. Die Trophäe ist 52 Zentimeter hoch, 5,7 Kilo schwer und fasst acht Liter Flüssigkeit. Bis ins Jahr 2015 feierte der FC Bayern 17 Pokalsiege, allein zehn im Berliner Olympiastadion.

BERLIN, MAY 17, 2014. Pure joy. After a 2–0 win vs. Dortmund, Brazilian Dante raises the DFB-Pokal to the Berlin night sky. The trophy is 52 cm tall, weighs 5.7 kg and holds 8 litres of liquid. As of 2015, Bayern has won the competition 17 times, including ten wins in the Olympiastadion.

FC BAYERN

MÜNCHEN, 23. MAI 2015. Die Feier der Deutschen Meisterschaft ist Jahr für Jahr der Höhepunkt der Saison. »Es ist der ehrlichste aller möglichen Titel«, hat Karl-Heinz Rummenigge einmal gesagt – weil er konstante Leistungen voraussetzt. Dieses Foto zeigt die Meisterschale getaucht in rot-weißes Konfetti. Als wenn die Schale und die bayerischen Vereinsfarben für immer verschmolzen wären …

MUNICH, MAY 23, 2015. The German championship party is the culmination of each season. "It's the most honest of all titles", Karl-Heinz Rummenigge once said – as it requires consistent performances over a whole year to achieve. This picture shows the Meisterschale immersed in red and white confetti, as if the trophy and Bayern's club colours were forever linked …

FREIBURG, 12. APRIL 2000. Oliver Kahn war das Inbild von Willensstärke und der Inbegriff von Emotionen. In Freiburg wurde er von einem Golfball an der Schläfe getroffen, musste anschließend von Manager Uli Hoeneß zurückgehalten werden. Trainer Hitzfeld forderte den Spielabbruch, aber Kahn spielte weiter. Die Bayern siegten 2:1.

FREIBURG, APRIL 12, 2000. Oliver Kahn was an epitome of willpower and emotion. In Freiburg he was absolutely and understandably livid after being hit by a golf ball. Still, he completed the game and Bayern won 2-1.

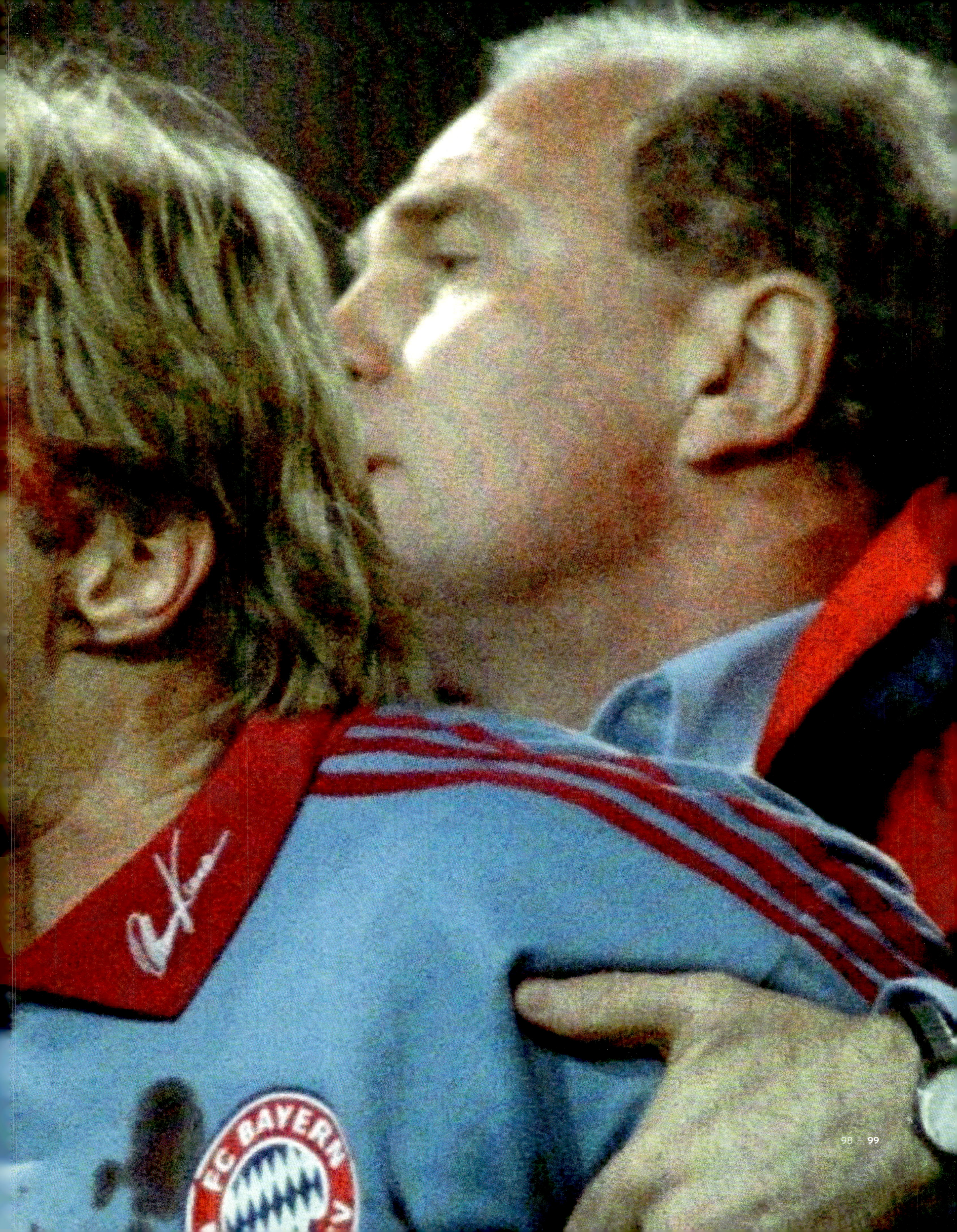
FC BAYERN

HAMBURG, 19. MAI 2001. Oliver Kahn schnappte sich am letzten Spieltag 2001 die Eckfahne im Hamburger Volksparkstadion nach dem Happy End im Meisterkrimi. In der allerletzten Sekunde der Nachspielzeit hatten die Bayern das 1:1 beim HSV erzielt und damit noch Schalke 04 abgefangen, das bereits den Titelgewinn gefeiert hatte. »Weiter, weiter, immer weiter« war Kahns Wahlspruch. Sein Nie-Aufgeben-Wollen wurde hier belohnt.

HAMBURG, MAY 19, 2001. Letting it all out: Oliver Kahn grabs the corner flag in Hamburg's Volksparkstadion. It is the final match day of the 2000-01 season and Bayern has just secured the championship in dramatic fashion with a stunning last-minute equalizer versus Hamburg, wresting the Meisterschale away from an already celebrating Schalke 04. "On and on and on", was Kahn's mantra. His never-say-die attitude was rewarded yet again.

MÜNCHEN, 25. MÄRZ 2000. Giovane Élber war stets für Überraschungen gut und ließ sich auch beim Torjubel immer wieder neue Choreografien einfallen. Beim 2:2 gegen den 1. FC Kaiserslautern erzielte er nicht nur beide Bayern-Tore, sondern animierte auch gleich noch drei Mitspieler zu einem übermütigen Kopfsprung. Roque Santa Cruz, Paulo Sergio und Sammy Kuffour hechten mit dem Doppeltorschützen der Auslinie entgegen. Vier Flieger für ein Tor.

MUNICH, MARCH 25, 2000. Giovane Élber was an imaginative player and frequently came up with creative ways to celebrate goals. In this 2-2 draw with Kaiserslautern he not only scored both goals for his side, he also persuaded three team mates to take a head-first dive in celebration. Roque Santa Cruz, Paulo Sergio and Sammy Kuffour take a plunge with the goal scorer, who just buried the equalizer to make it 2-2.

inental

MÜNCHEN, 17. JUNI 1987. Udo Lattek übermannen die Emotionen. Er zieht sich aus bis auf die Unterhose, gibt den Fans fast sein letztes Hemd: sein Abschiedsgeschenk nach seinem letzten Spiel als Bayern-Trainer. Mit seinem 14. Titel und der Deutschen Meisterschaft 1987 verabschiedet sich Deutschlands erfolgreichster Trainer aus München.

MUNICH, JUNE 17, 1987. Udo Lattek is overcome by emotions. He almost strips to the bones, literally giving the shirt off his back: his farewell gift to the fans after his last game as Bayern coach. With his 14th title and the 1987 championship, Germany's most prolific coach says goodbye to Munich.

KARLSRUHE, 23. SEPTEMBER 2007. Italienisch-französischer Doppeljubel: Mit den Verpflichtungen von Luca Toni und Franck Ribéry im Sommer 2007 leitete Bayern ein neues Zeitalter der Transferpolitik ein. Den beiden Stürmern bot sich bald genügend Anlass zum gemeinsamen Torjubel: wie hier im Spiel beim Karlsruher SC. Gern ließen sie sich dabei von den Fans feiern – und feierten sich so auch selbst.

KARLSRUHE, SEPTEMBER 23, 2007. Celebration in Italian and French: with the signings of Luca Toni and Franck Ribéry in the summer of 2007, Bayern heralded a new era in their transfer policy – to the obvious delight of their new stars as well as the fans.

MAILAND, 23. MAI 2001. Es herrscht Gänsehautstimmung im Giuseppe-Meazza-Stadion von Mailand. Zwei Jahre nach dem »Sekundentod« gegen Manchester United haben die Bayern mit Trainer Ottmar Hitzfeld wieder das Endspiel der Champions League erreicht. Die Choreografie der Bayern-Fans gibt ihrer Gefühlswelt Ausdruck. »Heute ist ein guter Tag, um Geschichte zu schreiben«, steht da zu lesen. Es wird ein guter Tag. Bayern schlägt Valencia im Elfmeterschießen.

MILAN, MAY 23, 2001. Goose bumps all around in Milan's Stadio Giuseppe Meazza. Two years after their devastating last-minute loss to Manchester United, Bayern and Ottmar Hitzfeld made it back to the final of the Champions League. The fans express their feelings with a stunning choreography. "Today is a good day to make history", it says on the banner. And it will be a good day, as Bayern defeats Valencia on penalties.

GESCHICHTE ZU SCHREIBEN!!!
NÖRDLINGEN
SINN
adidas
MOTOROLA
uefa.com
STEWARD

MÜNCHEN, 19. DEZEMBER 1998. Es sind besonders die Mittelstürmer, die Torjubel zu einem ihrer Markenzeichen machen. So wickelt sich etwa der immer für einen Spaß zu habende Brasilianer Giovane Élber nach einem Treffer gegen den VfL Wolfsburg in einen Werbeteppich ein. Torjubel ist die schönste Art der Freude und hat viele Facetten.

MUNICH, DECEMBER 19, 1998. It is especially the goal getters who seem to have a knack for coming up with trademark celebrations. Giovane Élber, always the prankster, wraps himself in an advertising rug after a goal against VfL Wolfsburg. Goal celebrations in their myriad forms are the cherry on the cake in football.

adidas
adidas

STUTTGART, 19. JUNI 1971. Udo Lattek brillierte als Motivator und glänzender Rhetoriker. Dass er auch Emotionen in sich trug, zeigt dieses Foto aus dem Jahr 1971. Der damals 36-jährige spätere Meistertrainer bewies Hochsprungqualitäten. Rechts neben ihm jubelt der etwas gesetztere Manager Robert Schwan über den Pokalsieg in Stuttgart. In der 118. Minute war Edgar Schneider der Siegtreffer zum 2:1 gegen den 1. FC Köln gelungen.

STUTTGART, JUNE 19, 1971. Udo Lattek was a brilliant motivator and rhetorician. This picture, taken during the 1971 German cup final, is evidence that he was also a pretty athletic fellow. The then 36-year-old bench boss demonstrates impressive high-jumping abilities. To his right, manager Robert Schwan delights in the cup win in Stuttgart. Edgar Schneider had scored the winner on 118 minutes, as Bayern defeated 1. FC Köln 2-1.

FRANKFURT, 1. MAI 1982. Die große Pokal-Liebe. Die Trophäe ist nicht gerade klein und auch von einigem Gewicht. Aber sie wird des Öfteren zärtlich liebkost und manchmal sogar mit ins Bett genommen. Hier streichelt Paul Breitner den DFB-Pokal liebevoll in der Kabine nach dem Gewinn 1982 gegen den 1. FC Nürnberg (4:2).

FRANKFURT, MAI 1, 1982. Cup love. The trophy isn't really small and rather heavy. Nevertheless, it is held tight, tenderly kissed, and sometimes even taken to bed. Here, Paul Breitner lovingly caresses it in the dressing room after Bayern's cup final win over Nuremberg (4-2) in 1982.

MÜNCHEN, 10. MÄRZ 1998. Nicht einmal drei Minuten dauerte der Auftritt von Giovanni Trapattoni. Aber die Worte, die er in italienisch-deutschem Stakkato nach dem Ausscheiden in der Champions League und einem 0:1 gegen Schalke in die Blöcke diktierte, wurden Kult. Kids auf der Straße adaptierten seine Sprüche und nahmen »Schwach wie Flasche leer« oder »Ich habe fertig« in ihren Sprachschatz auf. Auszüge: »Ein Trainer ist nicht ein Idiot! Ein Trainer sehen, was passieren in Platz. In diese Spiel es waren zwei, drei oder vier Spieler, die waren schwach wie Flasche leer!« ... »Struuunz! Strunz ist zwei Jahre hier, hat gespielt zehn Spiele, ist immer verletzt. Was erlauben Strunz?!« Und zum Ende die legendären Worte: »Ich habe fertig.«.

MUNICH, MARCH 10, 1998. It lasted not even three minutes, but Giovanni Trapattoni's temper tantrum in March 1998 is the stuff of legend. The coach lost it and ripped into his players after Bayern's elimination in the Champions League and a 0-1 defeat against Schalke in the Bundesliga,, but because the Italian's delivery was sprinkled with some droll phrases in broken German, the end result was – provided you were not one of his players – downright comical. Several of said phrases have long since entered popular culture, for example "Schwach wie Flasche leer" (Weak like bottle empty) or "Ich habe fertig" (I am finished). Some excerpts: "A coach is not an idiot! A coach seeing what happening on pitch. In this game it was two, three or four players, they were weak like bottle empty!" ... "Struuunz! Strunz is here for two years, has played ten games, is always injured. How dare Strunz?!" And finally the legendary words: "I am finished."

ANTENNE
BR

MÜNCHEN, 5. JUNI 1966. Im Autokorso zum Marienplatz – das hat in München Tradition. Schon beim Pokalsieg 1966 zeigen sich Kapitän Werner Olk, Trainer Tschik Cajkovski (mit Pokal), Manager Robert Schwan (rechts) und Präsident Wilhelm Neudecker (unten links) den begeisterten Münchnern.

MUNICH, JUNE 5, 1966. The motorcade to Marienplatz is a cherished tradition in Munich. After the 1966 German cup win, captain Werner Olk, coach Tschik Cajkovski (with the trophy), Manager Robert Schwan (right) and president Wilhelm Neudecker (below left) proudly make their way through the packed streets.

adidas
OPEL
OPE

MÜNCHEN, 24. MAI 1997. Kollektiver Torjubel. Nachdem Marcel Witeczek das 4:2 gegen den VfB Stuttgart erzielt hat, freuen sich Christian Ziege, Sammy Kuffour, Carsten Jancker und Christian Nerlinger (v. l.) mit dem Torschützen.

MUNICH, MAY 24, 1997. Players united in jubilation. After Marcel Witeczek made it 4-2 against VfB Stuttgart, team mates Christian Ziege, Sammy Kuffour, Carsten Jancker and Christian Nerlinger (from left to right) celebrate with the goal scorer.

MÜNCHEN, 2. APRIL 2002. Schauen Sie ihm in die Augen. Schauen Sie auf diese Körperhaltung. Stefan Effenberg demonstriert den bayerischen Siegeswillen. Gemeinsam mit Oliver Kahn ist er Anführer und Einpeitscher jener Bayern-Mannschaft, die 2001 die Champions League gewinnt. Im April 2002 heißt der Gegner Real Madrid. Bayern gewinnt das Hinspiel 2:1, scheidet aber nach einem 0:2 in Madrid im Viertelfinale aus. Hier feiert n Effenberg den Ausgleichstreffer zum 1:1 in München.

MUNICH, APRIL 2, 2002. Look at those eyes. Look at this posture. Stefan Effenberg demonstrates his will, the Bavarian will to win. He and Oliver Kahn are the co-leaders of a Bayern squad that wins the Champions League in 2001. In April 2002, Real Madrid are the opponents in the quarter-final. Bayern manage a 2-1 victory at home, but lose out to the Spaniards after a 0-2 defeat at the Bernabéu. Here Effenberg celebrates the equalizer that made it 1-1 in Munich.

KAHN
1

Akkus
SANYO
Batterien
AKKUS
SANYO

MÜNCHEN, 10. MAI 1997. Es war ein spontaner Wutausbruch und ein Akt der Enttäuschung. Giovanni Trapattoni hatte seinen Starstürmer Jürgen Klinsmann (14 Saisontore) im Heimspiel gegen den SC Freiburg ausgewechselt und den unbekannten Amateur Carsten Lakies gebracht. Da kam eine Werbetonne am Spielfeldrand gerade recht, in der Jürgen Klinsmann den Abdruck seines rechten Fußes hinterließ. Für den japanischen Batteriehersteller auf der Tonne war das beste Werbung. Das Stück wird heute in der »Erlebniswelt« ausgestellt.

MUNICH, MAY 10, 1997. It was a spontaneous outburst and an act of disappointment: against SC Freiburg Giovanni Trapattoni substituted his prominent striker Jürgen Klinsmann (14 goals on the season) in favour of unknown amateur Carsten Lakies. Klinsmann vented his anger with a right-footed kick to an advertising ton at the sidelines. The incident proved to be an inadvertent but welcome exposure for the Japanese battery manufacturer on the ton. Today it's possible to see the piece in the "Erlebniswelt".

ROM 21. OKTOBER 2014. Applaus im Gleichklang. Wenn Tausende von Menschen das Gleiche tun, ergibt sich ein ganz eigener Rhythmus. Die komplette Tribüne applaudiert hier der Mannschaft gegen den AS Rom und freut sich auf die Begegnung mit den Italienern in der Champions League.

ROME, OCTOBER 21, 2014. Applause in assonance. When thousands of people do the same thing, a distinctive rhythm emerges. A whole terrace applauds the team ahead of a matchup with AS Roma, looking forward to the Champions League.

BARCELONA, 26. MAI 1999. Fassungslosigkeit im Stadion Nou Camp von Barcelona. Das 1:2 gegen Manchester United im Finale der Champions League gilt in München als »Mutter aller Niederlagen«. Zwei Gegentore in der Nachspielzeit haben die Bayern ins Herz getroffen und sorgen für Reaktionen absoluter Niedergeschlagenheit bei den Spielern.

BARCELONA, MAY 26, 1999. Stunned disbelief in the Nou Camp in Barcelona. The 1–2 against Manchester United in the Champions League final has come to be known as the "mother of all defeats" in Munich. The two conceded goals in the final 120 seconds hurt deeply and entailed reactions of absolute depression.

MÜNCHEN, 16. AUGUST 2003. Claudio Pizarro wird von sechs Armen getragen. Der Peruaner ist der erfolgreichste Ausländer der Bundesliga mit den meisten Spielen und den meisten Toren. Neun Jahre stürmte »Pizza« in München und erzielte dabei 87 Bundesliga-Treffer.

MUNICH, AUGUST 16, 2003. Claudio Pizarro carried away on six arms. The Peruvian is the most prolific foreigner in Bundesliga history, with the most games and the most goals on his resume. In Munich, the striker played nine seasons, scoring 87 Bundesliga goals.

PARIS, 28. MAI 1975. »Mister Europacup« zeigt die begehrte Trophäe, den Europapokal der Landesmeister: Franz Roth ebnete den Weg zum 2:0-Sieg gegen Leeds United, erzielte das vorentscheidende 1:0 und setzte so die Finalserie der Bayern fort. Bis dahin hatten sie jedes Endspiel gewonnen.

PARIS, MAY 28, 1975. "Mister European Cup" presents the coveted trophy: Franz Roth paved the way for Bayern's 2-0 win over Leeds United, scoring the opening goal and ensuring the continuation of the club's impressive run: up to this point they had never lost a final.

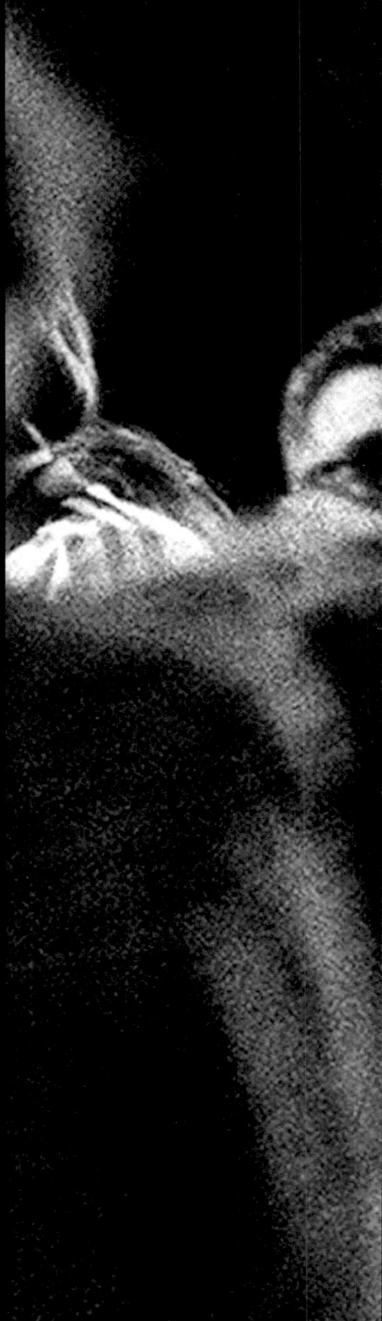

MÜNCHEN, 17. MAI 2008. Dürfen harte Männer weinen? Bei Ottmar Hitzfeld sind es Abschiedstränen, als er vor dem Spiel gegen Hertha BSC die Blumen von Manager Uli Hoeneß in Empfang nimmt. Nach fünf Meistertiteln hat er sich selbst zum Rückzug entschieden. Da sind Tränen der Wehmut erlaubt.

MUNICH, MAY 17, 2008. Boys don't cry... but grown men certainly do! Ottmar Hitzfeld cannot contain his emotions and lets the tears flow freely. For the long-time head coach, they are tears of goodbye in the wake of his final game with FCB versus Hertha BSC in 2008. With five championships, Hitzfeld is one of Bayern's most prolific coaches.

DIE POPULARITÄT STEIGT UND STEIGT
EVER INCREASING POPULARITY

Nein, der FC Bayern München lässt keinen Fußballfan kalt. Entweder man mag ihn oder man mag ihn nicht. Mag sein, dass diese Polarisierung mit den vielen Erfolgen zusammenhängt. Aber auch Neid muss man sich erarbeiten. Mag auch sein, dass das zur Schau gestellte »Mia san mia«-Gefühl als Arroganz ausgelegt wird. Mag ebenfalls sein, dass sich längst nicht jeder Fußballfan mit der bayerischen Lebensart identifizieren kann. Aber die Schar derer, die sich zum FC Bayern bekennen, nimmt schwindelerregende Höhen an:

– Der FC Bayern hat über 250.000 Mitglieder und ist damit vor Benfica Lissabon der größte Sportverein der Welt.

– Der FC Bayern wird unterstützt von mehr als 4.000 Fanklubs mit über 300.000 Mitgliedern. Das reicht von Flensburg bis Kiefersfelden, von Schanghai bis Mombasa, von den Philippinen bis in den Iran – organisierte Bayern-Fans gibt es weltweit.

Und die Popularität wächst und wachst…

In den 1970er Jahren war der SSV Ulm mit seinen knapp 10.000 Mitgliedern Deutschlands größter Sportverein. Im Jahr 2000 zählte der FC Bayern bereits 91.288 Mitglieder, 2005 waren es 120.000, 2010 bereits 171.000, und im Jahr 2012 wurde die magische 200.000er-Marke geknackt. Der FC Bayern fördert die enge Verbindung zu Mitgliedern und Fanklubs. Mit Raimond Aumann ist auch hier ein ehemaliger Profi und Weltmeister dafür verantwortlich, so wie es der FC Bayern immer verstanden hat, verdiente Spieler in die Klubarbeit zu integrieren.

Trotz der steigenden Kommerzialisierung und des Wachstums zu einem Global Player pflegt der Rekordmeister die Basis. Jedes Jahr in der Vorweihnachtszeit besucht jeder Profi einen Fanklub – ein Dankeschön für die Unterstützung.

Freude – dieses Wort zählt zu den Bayern-Werten und ist damit Bestandteil der Klubphilosophie. Wer nicht mit Freude zum Training geht, wer nicht mit Vorfreude in die Allianz Arena einläuft, kann keine Freude ernten und

It's safe to say that no football fan is indifferent to FC Bayern München. You either like them or you don't. The polarisation may very well be a consequence of the many successes the club achieved. It takes a lot of hard work, however, to earn envy, and envy, of course, is the best form of flattery. It may be that the oft-repeated "mia san mia" sentiment is mistaken by some as arrogance. And it may be that not every football fan can relate to the Bavarian lifestyle. But the number of people who actively support FC Bayern is reaching staggering heights:

– FC Bayern has more than 250,000 members, making it the biggest football club in the world ahead of Benfica Lisbon.

– FC Bayern is supported by more than 4,000 fan clubs with 300,000 registered members or more, from Flensburg to Kiefersfelden, from Shanghai to Mombasa, from the Philippines to Iran – Bayern fans are organised all over the world.

And the club's popularity is ever increasing …

Back in the 1970s SSV Ulm was the biggest club in Germany with 10,000 members. In 2000 Bayern already boasted 91,288 members. By 2005 that number had increased to 120,000, 2010 it was 171,000, and in 2012 the club cracked the magic number of 200,000. FC Bayern fosters a tight bond between members and fan clubs. This is the area of work of former number one goalkeeper and world champion Raimond Aumann, who, like so many ex Bayern pros, is still involved in club operations and today serves as supporters and fan club coordinator.

Despite the increasing commercialisation of the game and its establishment as a global player, the record champion maintains a strong connection to the base. Every year at the start of the Christmas season each player pays a visit to a fan club by way of thanks for their support.

Joy is a cherished value for Bayern and thus an element of the club's philosophy. If a player does not feel joy at practice or when he runs onto the pitch of the Allianz Arena, he cannot reap joy in return nor can he convey

keine Freude vermitteln. Der Funken muss vom Rasen auf die Ränge überspringen. Denn die Fans garantieren die Gänsehautatmosphäre in der Arena und sorgen somit für das berühmte Stadionerlebnis. Unvergleichlich sind die verschiedenen Choreografien, die Bayerns Fanklubs auf die Tribünen zaubern. Allen voran jene im Champions-League-Finale 2001 gegen den FC Valencia: »Heute ist ein guter Tag, um Geschichte zu schreiben«, stand da zu lesen.

Wer Freude verbreitet, muss Emotionen zeigen. Dazu gehören auch Gefühlsregungen, wie sie Oliver Kahn eigen sind. Unvergessen die Szene, als er nach dem kaum mehr für möglich gehaltenen Tor gegen Hamburg am letzten Spieltag die Meisterschaft 2001 feiert. »Weiter, weiter, immer weiter«, hat Kahn nach der »Mutter aller Niederlagen«, dem K.o. im Champions-League-Finale 1999 gegen Manchester United in letzter Sekunde, ausgerufen und sich selbst daran gehalten. Nie aufgeben, kämpfen bis zur letzten Sekunde. Diese Haltung, die er auch seiner Mannschaft vermittelte, lebte Kahn seit den denkwürdigen Minuten von Barcelona 1999 in jedem neuen Spiel, in das er nun ging. Kein Wunder also, dass sich wieder große Erfolge für den FC Bayern und seinen Torhüter einstellten. Und wenn wir nach diesen Triumphen in das Gesicht von Oliver Kahn schauen, sehen wir die pure Freude, die emotionale Entladung.

Auch Wut ist eine emotionale Regung. Die Wutrede von Giovanni Trapattoni ist ebenso legendär wie der Tonnentritt von Jürgen Klinsmann oder die Rede von Franz Beckenbauer nach einer 0:3-Niederlage in Lyon, als er der Mannschaft »Altherrenfußball« attestierte und empfahl, die Berufswahl zu überdenken. Die Spieler antworteten, wie es sich für den FC Bayern gehört. Weil sie sich bei der Ehre gepackt fühlten, gingen sie bis an ihre Grenzen – und gewannen anschließend die Champions League.

Nein, der FC Bayern lässt keinen kalt. Und weil diese Mannschaft durch schönen Fußball so viel Freude bereitet, steigt auch die Zahl ihrer Freunde. Bayern ist »in«. Weiteres Wachstum inbegriffen.

joy to the fans. The spark has to jump from the pitch to the stands, as it is the fans with their chants and choreographies that create the atmosphere in the arena and make the game such a unique experience. Like it said on the memorable banner Bayern fans unrolled ahead of the 2001 Champions League final against Valencia: “Today is a good day to make history”.

To convey joy you need to display your emotions. Few players wore their heart on their sleeve the way Oliver Kahn did. There is an image that will always stick in the mind: Kahn celebrating the German championship in 2001 after Bayern’s last-minute goal versus Hamburg on match day 34. But he also always rallied his team, just like he did after the mother of all defeats, the sudden death in the 1999 Champions League final versus Manchester United. Never say die was Kahn’s mantra and he was always giving his all until the final second. It was this attitude Kahn lived since the memorable minutes of Barcelona in each new match he played ever after – and that he drummed into his team mates’ minds. No wonder FC Bayern and its goalkeeper hadn’t to wait long for new triumphs. And look then at Oliver Kahn’s face at the finale whistle and what you see is emotional release, pure and utter joy.

Another powerful emotion is rage. Examples include Giovanni Trapattoni’s infamous temper tantrum, Klinsmann kicking a ton or Franz Beckenbauer’s dressing down after a brutal 0–3 loss in Lyon, where he accused the team of playing like old men and suggested changing profession. Thus provoked, the players responded with a run of exceptional performances and went on to win the Champions League.

No, Bayern does not leave anyone cold. And because the team brings joy with their beautiful football, the number of friends and fans is ever increasing. Bayern’s popularity is unmatched and it keeps on growing.

»Das Besondere an der Bayern-Familie: Wenn du einmal dabei warst, wirst du nie fallen gelassen. Ich bin stolz darauf, dass ich zu dieser Familie seit meiner Jugend gehören darf.«
HANS-GEORG »KATSCHE« SCHWARZENBECK

"This is what makes the Bayern family something so special: once you have been a part of it, they will never let you down. I'm proud to have been allowed to be a part of this family ever since my youth."
HANS-GEORG "KATSCHE" SCHWARZENBECK

Es sind viele Protagonisten, die diesem Klub zu Weltruhm verholfen haben. Die Weltmeister, die Superstars, die Ausländer und auch die Trainer, die den FC Bayern zu dem gemacht haben, was er heute ist.

They are the main protagonists who established the club's renown and recognition. The world champions, the superstars, the players from abroad and the coaches, that helped to make Bayern what it is today.

MÜNCHEN, 9. JUNI 1973. Franz Beckenbauer, der Libero. Der begnadete Techniker spielte von 1964 bis 1977 für die Bayern. Er galt als weltbester Fußballer, begann die Karriere als Linksaußen und erfand später die Libero-Position. Hier war er Abwehrchef und Spielmacher in einer Person. Dieses Foto diente als Plakat für den Film »Der Libero«.

MUNICH, JUNE 9, 1973. Franz Beckenbauer, the Sweeper. The gifted and elegant technician played for Bayern from 1964 to 1977. He was considered the best player in the world and, after starting his career as a left winger, basically redefined the role of the sweeper, taking care of the defence while also joining the attack. This picture served as a poster for the movie "Der Libero" (The Sweeper).

Fussball

DEUTSCHER FUSSBALLMEISTER
FIFA

MÜNCHEN, 14. SEPTEMBER 2015. Der Vorstandsvorsitzende im Kreis seiner Pokale: Karl-Heinz Rummenigge prägt den FC Bayern seit 1976, erst als Spieler, seit 1991 in der Vereinsführung. 1980 und 1981 wurde der Weltklassestürmer zu »Europas Fußballer des Jahres« gewählt, seit 2002 ist er Vorstandsvorsitzender der FC Bayern AG. In seiner Sammlung fehlt keine Trophäe.

MUNICH, SEPTEMBER 14, 2015. The chief executive officer and his trophies: Karl-Heinz Rummenigge has shaped Bayern since 1976, first as a player and since 1991 as an executive. In 1980 and 1981 the world class striker was named "European Footballer of the Year", since 2002 he served FC Bayern AG in his current position.

MÜNCHEN, 1. OKTOBER 2007. Franck Ribéry ist längst in München heimisch geworden. Seit 2007 stürmt der kleine Franzose für den FC Bayern und erlebte hier seine größten Triumphe. Schon kurz nach seiner Ankunft posierte er in der zünftigen Landestracht.

MUNICH, OCTOBER 1, 2007. Franck Ribéry feels right at home in Munich. The smallish Frenchman joined FC Bayern in 2007 and got to celebrate numerous triumphs with the team. Only shortly after his arrival he posed in traditional attire.

HAMBURG, 13. MÄRZ 1999. Die Köpfe verschmelzen, die Arme ergeben ein synchrones Bild. Samuel Kuffour im Kopfballduell mit dem Hamburger Anthony Yeboah.

HAMBURG, MARCH 13, 1999. The heads appear to merge, the arms synchronised. Samuel Kuffour in an aerial duel with Hamburg's Anthony Yeboah.

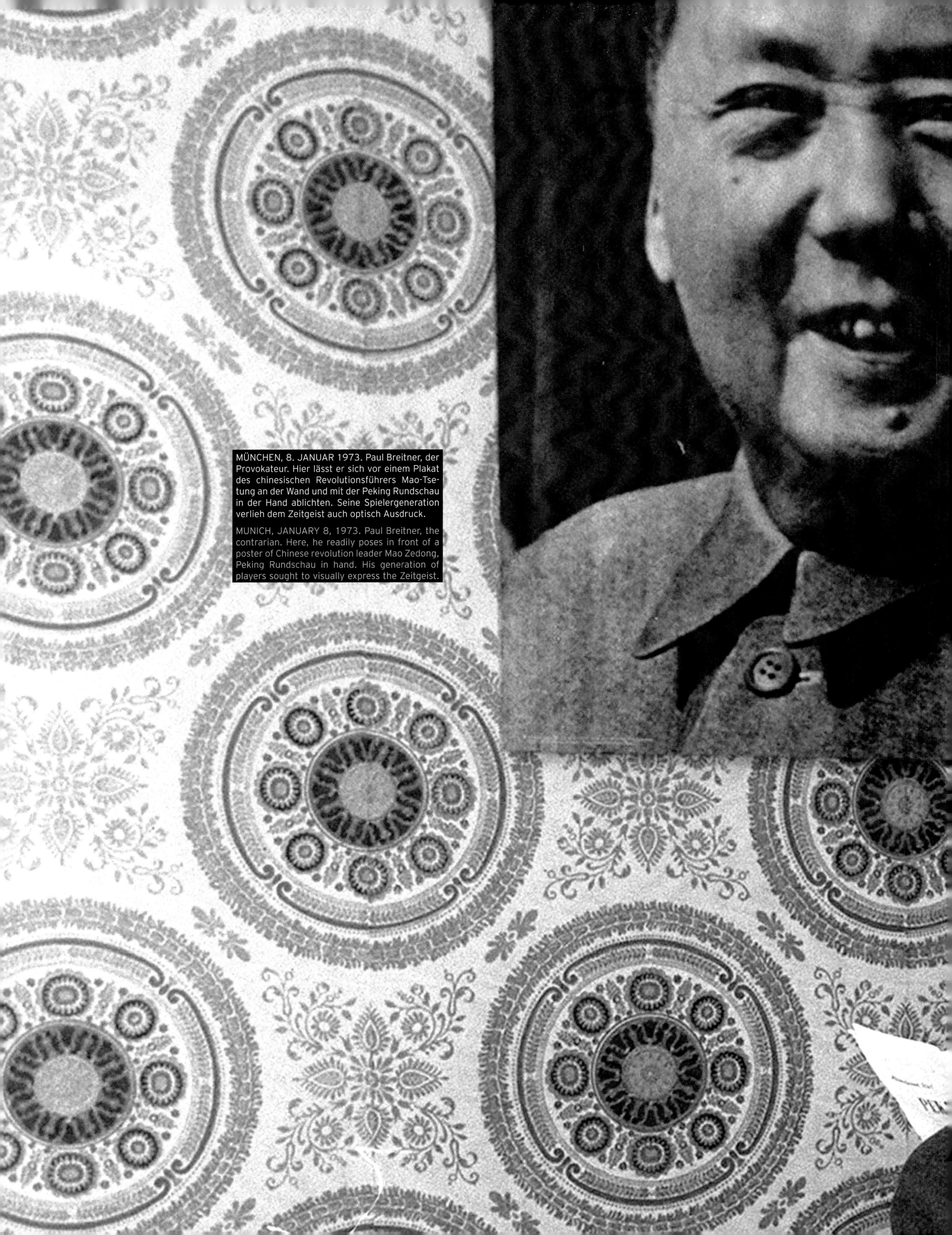

MÜNCHEN, 8. JANUAR 1973. Paul Breitner, der Provokateur. Hier lässt er sich vor einem Plakat des chinesischen Revolutionsführers Mao-Tse-tung an der Wand und mit der Peking Rundschau in der Hand ablichten. Seine Spielergeneration verlieh dem Zeitgeist auch optisch Ausdruck.

MUNICH, JANUARY 8, 1973. Paul Breitner, the contrarian. Here, he readily poses in front of a poster of Chinese revolution leader Mao Zedong, Peking Rundschau in hand. His generation of players sought to visually express the Zeitgeist.

PEKING 17
RUNDSCHAU
Zusammenkunft des Vorsitzenden
Mao mit Präsident Echeverria

MÜNCHEN, 1. AUGUST 1969. Gerd Müller, »Bomber der Nation« und König der Tore. Seine 365 Bundesliga-Treffer aus 427 Spielen sind ein Rekord für die Ewigkeit. Die Quote von 68 Toren in 62 Länderspielen ist noch beeindruckender. 1970 und 1972 war er bester Torschütze Europas, siebenmal wurde er Torschützenkönig der Bundesliga – mit der Rekordzahl von 40 Treffern in der Saison 1971/72.

MUNICH, AUGUST 1, 1969. Gerd Müller, the "Bomber" and king of goals. His 365 Bundesliga goals in 427 matches are a record for the ages. His tally of 68 goals in 62 caps for Germany is even more impressive. Müller won the European Golden Boot as the leading goal scorer in domestic matches in 1970 and 1972 and seven times was the Bundesliga top scorer. His 40 goals in 1971-72 remain a record to this day.

MÖNCHENGLADBACH, 18. MAI 2013. Die Führungs-Troika steht für Kontinuität und Volksnähe. Karl Hopfner, hier mit Uli Hoeneß und Kalle Rummenigge auf der Tribüne, übernahm bereits 1983 die Geschäftsführung, ist seit 2014 Präsident und Aufsichtsratsvorsitzender. Zudem vertritt er die Bayern Vorstand der Deutschen Fußball Liga und in UEFA-Gremien.

MÖNCHENGLADBACH, MAY 18, 2013. Bayern's leadership troika stands for continuity and down-to-earthness. Karl Hopfner, seen here beside Uli Hoeneß and Kalle Rummenigge in the stands, assumed the role of Bayern's managing director in 1983 and since 2014 serves as the club's president and chairman of the board. In addition, he represents Bayern as a member of the board of the Deutsche Fußball Liga as well as in various UEFA commissions.

MÜNCHEN, 1. JUNI 1975. Dettmar Cramer als Napoleon. Am 16. Januar 1975 kam er zum FC Bayern, wurde zweifacher Europacup- (1975 und 1976) und Weltpokalsieger. Der Fußball-Professor Dettmar Cramer erhielt wegen seiner Körpergröße von nur 1,61 Meter den Spitznamen »Napoleon« und ließ sich im Sommer 1975 von Diana Sandmann, der damaligen Lebensgefährtin Franz Beckenbauers, in der entsprechenden Kostümierung ablichten.

MUNICH, JUNE 1, 1975. Dettmar Cramer as Napoleon. He joined Bayern on January 16, 1975, and led the club to two European Cups (1975 and 1976) and the Intercontinental Cup. He was nicknamed "football professor" and, because of his diminutive stature, "Napoleon". The photo was taken in the summer of 1975 by Franz Beckenbauer's then-partner Diana Sandmann.

MÜNCHEN, 15. AUGUST 1968. Eleganz und Perfektion am Ball. Auch in Frack und Zylinder macht der junge Beckenbauer eine gute Figur. Schon im Alter von 22 Jahren gibt er für deutsche Fotografen ein äußerst begehrtes Motiv ab.

MUNICH, AUGUST 15, 1968. Franz Beckenbauer exuded elegance and perfection on the pitch, but he also cut a fine figure in tail coat and top hat. At the tender age of 22 he was already one of the most coveted subjects for photographers across Germany.

MÜNCHEN, 4. JUNI 2013. Uli Hoeneß auf dem Gipfel, mit Europapokal, Supercup, Meisterschale und DFB-Pokal. Seit 1970 ist er beim FC Bayern, als Spieler (bis 1979), als Manager (bis 2009), dann als Vereinspräsident und Vorsitzender des Aufsichtsrats der FC Bayern München AG. Er hat insgesamt 54 Titel gewonnen, darunter 36 in seiner Zeit als Manager. Hoeneß gilt als Seele des Vereins.

MUNICH, JUNE 4, 2013. Uli Hoeneß on top, with European Cup, Super Cup, Meisterschale and German cup. Hoeneß served Bayern since 1970, first as a player (until 1979), later as general manager (until 2009), and eventually as president and chairman of the supervisory board of FC Bayern München AG. In all, and including his stint as general manager, he has won 54 titles. Hoeneß is regarded as the heart and soul of the club.

MAINZ, 20. JANUAR 2004. Zur Jahrtausendwende wählten die Bayern-Fans ihre Jahrhundertelf. Der kleine Franzose gehörte dazu: Bixente Lizarazu hatte sich in ihre Herzen gespielt. Der Linksverteidiger wurde 1998 Weltmeister und zwei Jahre später Europameister. Mit dem FC Bayern gewann er 18 Titel – er ist damit Bayerns erfolgreichster Ausländer.

MAINZ, JANUARY 20, 2004. When Bayern fans voted for their team of the century, the smallish Frenchman made the cut: Bixente Lizarazu will always hold a special place in their hearts. The left back from the Basque Country was part of the French team that won the 1998 World Cup and the European championship two years later. Lizarazu won 18 titles with Bayern, making him the most successful foreign player in club history.

T-Mobile

MÜNCHEN, 15. APRIL 1990. Fototermin zum 90-jährigen Vereinsjubiläum: Jupp Heynckes lässt sich von seinem Assistenten Egon Coordes den Zylinder zurechtrücken. In historischem Frack begibt sich der Trainer auf die Zeitreise zurück ins Jahr 1900. Als Trainer prägte er zwei Bayern-Epochen mit insgesamt fünf Titeln.

MUNICH, APRIL 15, 1990. Photo session for the club's 90th anniversary: assistant Egon Coordes lends a helping hand to Jupp Heynckes. In top hat and tail coat, the head coach travels back in time to the year 1900. Heynckes shaped two eras in the club's history, winning five titles.

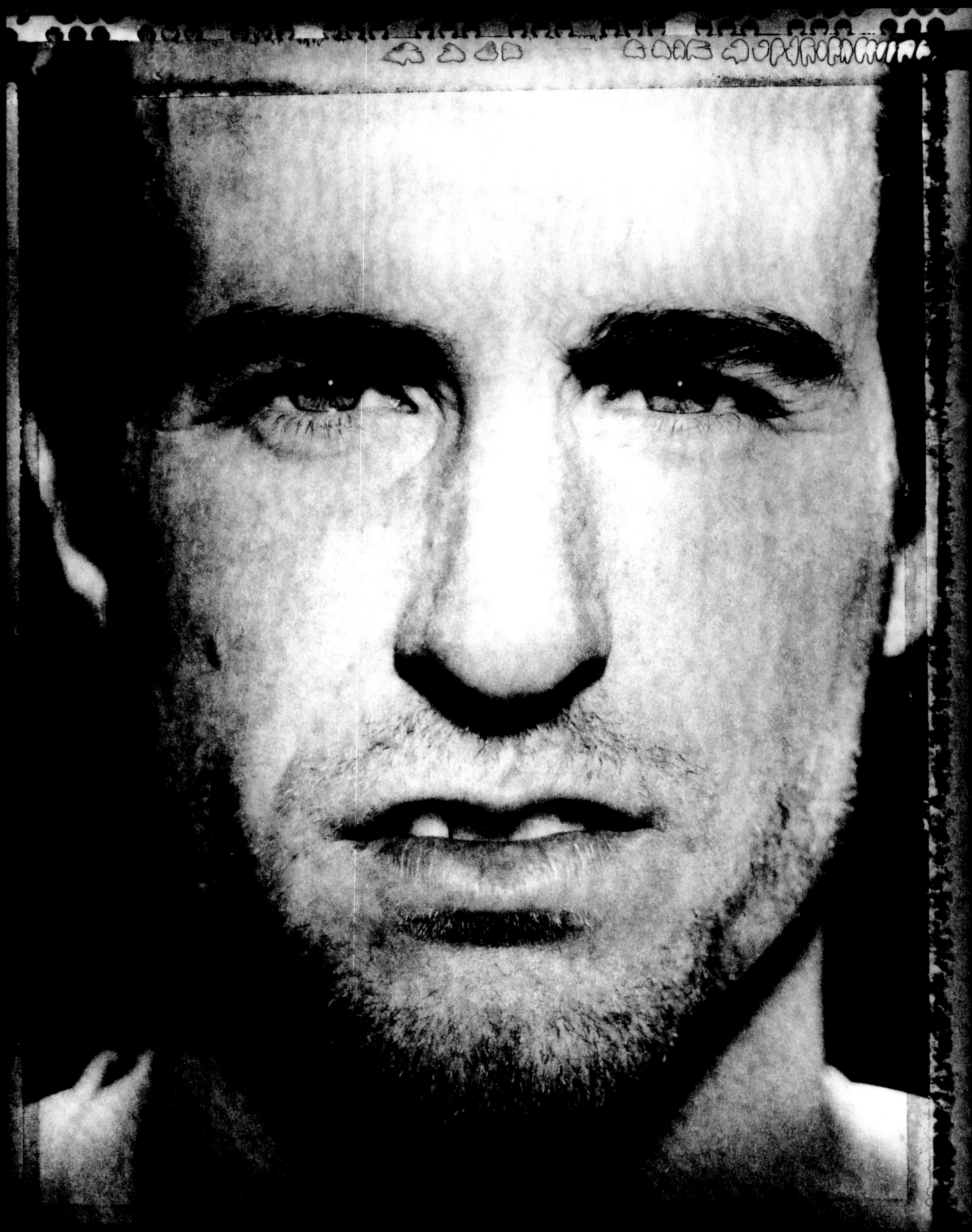

MÜNCHEN, 19 JUNI 2003. Mehmet Scholl, der Verwandlungskünstler. Der stets zu Späßen aufgelegte Teeny-Schwarm ist mit 21 Titeln einer der erfolgreichsten Bayern-Profis. Bei seinem Abschiedsspiel 2007 wurde er zum Ehrenspieler ernannt und übergab seine Rückennummer 7 an Franck Ribéry.

MUNICH, JUNE 19, 2003. Mehmet Scholl, man of many faces. With 21 titles, the heartthrob and notorious prankster is one of the most prolific players in club history. At his farewell match against Barcelona in 2007, he was named honorary player and passed his jersey number 7 on to Franck Ribéry.

MÜNCHEN, 27. FEBRUAR 2015. Ein Abwehrspieler in geradezu ästhetisch anmutender Haltung. Jérôme Boateng schwebt in der Luft, verschafft sich dank ausgebreiteter Arme die nötige Balance. Und hat die Augen vorbildlich auf den Ball gerichtet.

MUNICH, FEBRUARY 27, 2015. A defender with a flair for aesthetics. Jérôme Boateng hovers in the air, arms outstretched for better balance, eyes on the ball. A striking figure.

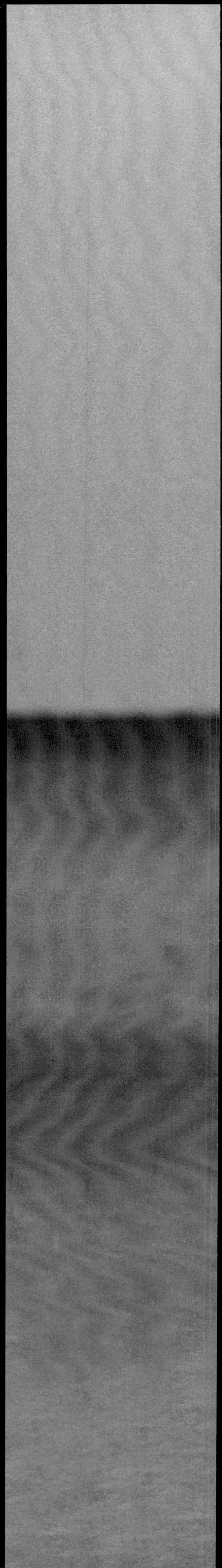

MÜNCHEN, 12. MAI 1977. Sepp Maier, der Entertainer. Die Torwartlegende galt nicht nur als weltbeste Nummer eins, sondern war auch als Spaßvogel bekannt. Im Stadion hechtete Maier mal einer Flugente hinterher, während Paul Breitner gerade einen Elfmeter verwandelte. Hier zeigt er sich verkleidet als legendärer bayerischer Komiker Karl Valentin.

MUNICH, MAY 12, 1977. Sepp Maier, the Entertainer. Bayern icon Sepp Maier was not only considered the best goalkeeper of his time, he also earned a reputation as a notorious jokester. He once chased a duck during a game while Paul Breitner was taking a penalty. Here Maier is dressed as legendary Bavarian comedian Karl Valentin.

STARNBERG, 1. MAI 2004. Die Haare hängen wild ins Gesicht, die Augen sind fokussiert: Michael Ballack, der die Rückennummer 13 zu seinem Markenzeichen machte, prägte das Spiel der Bayern zwischen 2002 und 2006, wurde in dieser Zeit dreimal zu Deutschlands Fußballer des Jahres gewählt und galt als einer der besten Mittelfeldspieler Europas.

STARNBERG, MAY 1, 2004. Hair ruffled, eyes focussed: Michael Ballack, whose number 13 became his signature, shaped Bayern's play between 2002 and 2006. He was named Germany's Footballer of the Year three times and considered one of the finest midfielders in Europe.

MÜNCHEN, 1971. Das Foto spielt natürlich auf seinen Spitznamen an. Franz Roth, Bauernsohn aus Memmingen, wurde »Bulle« genannt – aufgrund seiner Kraft und der Gewalt seiner Schüsse, für die im Training einmal eine Geschwindigkeit von 137 km/h gemessen wurde. In drei Europapokal-Endspielen schoss er jeweils das 1:0.

MUNICH, 1971. The photo hints at how Franz Roth, a farmer's son from Memmingen, earned his nickname. He was called "Bulle" (bull) due to his strength and powerful shot, which was once clocked in practice at 137 km/h. Roth was known to come up big in crucial matches, scoring the opening goal in three European Cup finals.

MÜNCHEN, 11. MAI 1981. Katsche Schwarzenbeck, der Putzer. Hans-Georg, genannt »Katsche«, Schwarzenbeck stand oft im Schatten der Superstars. Aber als er zum Karriereende 1981 die von ihm gewonnenen Trophäen präsentierte, ergab sich eine stolze Sammlung: sechsmal Deutscher Meister, dreimal DFB-Pokalsieger, vier Europapokal-Triumphe, Weltpokalgewinner, Europameister und Weltmeister. Er wurde »Putzer vom Kaiser« genannt, weil er neben dem eleganten Libero Beckenbauer als Vorstopper für das Grobe zuständig war.

MUNICH, MAY 11, 1981. Katsche Schwarzenbeck, the Kaiser's Bodyguard. Hans-Georg, called "Katsche", Schwarzenbeck stood somewhat in the shadows of the superstars. Yet when he finished his career in 1981, he had amassed quite an impressive collection of silverware: six Bundesliga titles, three German cup wins, four European Cup wins, an Intercontinental Cup plus a European Championship and a World Cup. He was known as the "Kaiser's bodyguard", covering as centre back for Beckenbauer, whenever the elegant sweeper joined the attack.

MÜNCHEN, 25. AUGUST 2015. Der Irokesenschnitt ist sein Markenzeichen: Arturo Vidal gilt als vorbildlicher Fighter, gewann mit Chile die Copa América und stand mit Juventus Turin im Finale der Champions League. Seit Sommer 2015 ist der Mittelfeldspieler beim FC Bayern.

MUNICH, AUGUST 25, 2015. The mohawk is his signature: Arturo Vidal is hailed as a true warrior, has won the Copa América with Chile and also reached the Champions League final with Juventus Turin. The midfielder joined Bayern in the summer of 2015.

MÜNCHEN, 10. SEPTEMBER 1976. Schnappschuss aus dem Olympiastadion: Manager Robert Schwan mit Pfeife und typischer Schiebermütze, daneben Trainer Dettmar Cramer. Das 9:0 gegen Tennis Borussia Berlin scheint eher zu langweilen.

MUNICH, SEPTEMBER 10, 1976. A snapshot from the Olympiastadion: manager Robert Schwan with pipe and trademark flat cap, next to him coach Dettmar Cramer. The 9-0 versus Tennis Borussia Berlin fails to excite these gentlemen.

LEVERKUSEN, 17. JULI 1999. Waagerecht legt sich Paulo Sergio in die Luft und versucht im Ligapokal-Finale 1999 gegen Bremen einen akrobatischen Seitfallzieher. Dass er den Ball verfehlt, wird aber zur Nebensache. Denn die Bayern gewinnen nach einem 2:1 ihren ersten Titel in der Saison 1999/2000.

LEVERKUSEN, JULY 17, 1999. Paulo Sergio attempts an acrobatic scissor kick in the 1999 Ligacup final. Never mind that he misses the ball, it's still a sight to behold. Bayern, however, win their first title in the 1999-2000 season after a 2-1 versus Bremen.

NÜRNBERG, 12. JUNI 1932. Der erste Meistertitel. Über 50.000 Zuschauer kamen ins Städtische Stadion von Nürnberg, darunter 500 arbeitslose Radfahrer aus München, vom FC Bayern mit Freikarten ausgestattet. Bayern siegte durch Tore von Mittelstürmer Oskar Rohr (36., Handelfmeter) und Franz Krumm (75.) gegen die Frankfurter Eintracht und nahm Revanche für die zuvor erlittene Niederlage im Kampf um die Süddeutsche Meisterschaft.

NUREMBERG, JUNE 12, 1932. The first championship. More than 50,000 spectators flocked to the Städtisches Stadion in Nuremberg, including 500 unemployed cyclists from Munich, who had received free tickets from Bayern. FCB prevailed on goals by centre forward Oskar Rohr (36., penalty) and Franz Krumm (75.) against Eintracht Frankfurt.

MÜNCHEN, 27. FEBRUAR 1900. Franz Adolf Louis John, Fotograf aus Pritzwalk, war der erste Präsident des FC Bayern. Mit zehn weiteren Fußballern trat er aus dem Turnverein MTV 1879 München aus und gründete im Restaurant »Gisela« den Fußballverein FC Bayern. Auf seinem Grab im Berliner Stadtteil Pankow erinnert ein Gedenkstein an seine Verdienste.

MUNICH, FEBRUARY 27, 1900. Franz Adolf Louis John, a photographer from Pritzwalk, was the club's first president. Along with 10 other kindred spirits he quit the gymnastics club MTV 1879 München and, in the restaurant "Gisela", founded the football club FC Bayern. His accomplishments are commemorated with a memorial stone on his grave in Berlin's borough of Pankow.

MÜNCHEN, 12. JUNI 1932. Kurt Landauer war viermal Präsident des Vereins: 1913/14, von 1919 bis 1921, von 1922 bis 1933 und 1947 bis 1951. Im Jahr 1939 musste der jüdische Kaufmann in die Schweiz fliehen. Unter ihm gelang der sportliche Aufstieg mit zwei süddeutschen (1926 und 1928) und der ersten Deutschen Meisterschaft 1932. Nach dem Zweiten Weltkrieg baute er den Verein wieder auf und erwarb für ihn das Gelände an der Säbener Straße, bis heute die Heimat des FC Bayern.

MUNICH, JUNE 12, 1932. Kurt Landauer was four times Bayern's president: in 1913/14, from 1919 till 1921, from 1922 to 1933, and from 1947 to 1951. In 1939 the Jewish merchant had to flee to Switzerland. During his second stint, the club won two Southern German championships (1926 and 1928) as well as their first German championship in 1932. After the war Landauer rebuilt the club and acquired the grounds at Säbener Strasse, home of FC Bayern to this day.

FC BAYERN MÜNCHEN
FIFA

MÜNCHEN, 5. NOVEMBER 2014. Vier Beine und zwei Hände: Manuel Neuer gilt als weltbester Torhüter. Furchtlos wirft er sich hier dem Angreifer des AS Rom entgegen, den Ball stets mit den Augen fixierend. Neuer hat das Torwartspiel revolutioniert und glänzt heute als elfter Feldspieler.

MUNICH, NOVEMBER 5, 2014. Four legs, two hands: Manuel Neuer is considered to be the best goalkeeper in the world. Here, he fearlessly confronts the striker of AS Roma, eyes fixed on the ball. Neuer revolutionised the goalkeeper's game and now shines as an 11th outfield player.

MÜNCHEN, 17. JUNI 1989. Die Augen blicken auf die Schale, das Gesicht verklärt ein seliges Lächeln. Klaus Augenthaler prägte als Libero und Kapitän mit sieben Meistertiteln und drei Pokalsiegen eine Ära bei den Bayern. Nach dem 5:0 gegen Bochum am letzten Spieltag der Saison 1988/89 darf die Champagnerflasche mit ins Entmüdungsbecken.

MUNICH, JUNE 17, 1989. A glimpse at the trophy puts a big smile on his face: as the team's sweeper and skipper, Klaus Augenthaler shaped an era at Bayern, winning seven Bundesliga titles and three German cups. A 5-0 win over Bochum on the last match day of the 1988-89 season was a fine occasion for a sip of champagne in the relaxation bath.

LONDON, 25. MAI 2013. Der Kapitän schreit seine Freude in die Londoner Nacht. Endlich hat er mit seinen Bayern auch die Champions League gewonnen. Der Abwehr-Allrounder ist geborener Münchener, kam im Alter von zwölf Jahren vom FT Gern zu den Bayern und übernahm im Januar 2011 die Kapitänsbinde.

LONDON, MAY 25, 2013. The captain screams with joy in the London night. He f nally won the Champions League with Bayern. The versatile defender was born in Munich, joined the club from FT Gern at age 12, and was appointed the team's skipper in 2011.

FINAL WEMBLEY 2013

adidas

MÜNCHEN, 28. NOVEMBER 1998. Auch Köpfe sind manchmal kopflos. Hasan Salihamidzic, von 1998 bis 2007 in Diensten des FC Bayern, versteckt sein Haupt nach einem 2:0-Heimsieg gegen den 1. FC Nürnberg.

MUNICH, NOVEMBER 28, 1998. Hardly headless: Hasan Salihamidzic, who played for Bayern from 1998 to 2007, hides his head after a 2-0 win at home against Nuremberg.

DREI WELTSTARS AM SCHALTPULT
THREE LEGENDS AT THE HELM

Wer den FC Bayern verstehen will, muss sich eine Aufstellung von 1976 ansehen. Im Hampden Park von Glasgow bestritt der FC Bayern das dritte Finale in Serie im Europapokal der Landesmeister: Der Gegner hieß AS Saint-Étienne. Die Bayern gewannen den Titel an diesem 12. Mai zum dritten Mal nacheinander durch den 1:0-Siegtreffer von Franz »Bulle« Roth (57.). Der Kapitän hieß Franz Beckenbauer, mit seinen 30 Jahren ein Weltstar und unumstrittener Bayern-Boss. Im Angriff wirbelte der pfeilschnelle Weltmeister Uli Hoeneß, mit 24 Jahren in der Blüte seiner Karriere. Auf rechts gab ein Greenhorn sein Finaldebüt: Karl-Heinz Rummenigge griff bereits mit nur 20 Jahren an den berühmten Henkelpott.

Beckenbauer – Hoeneß – Rummenigge: drei Weltstars, die bis heute den FC Bayern prägen. Hoeneß war es, der später Karl-Heinz Rummenigges Transfer zu Inter Mailand managte. Und als Rummenigge 1986 als Kapitän Vizeweltmeister wurde, hieß der Teamchef Franz Beckenbauer. Diese Achse, die 1976 den französischen Meister zum Verlierer machte, startete in der Führungsetage des FC Bayern eine zweite Karriere. Uli Hoeneß wechselte zum 1. Mai 1979 die Seiten und wurde mit 27 Jahren der jüngste Manager der Bundesliga-Geschichte. Um die sportliche Kompetenz im Verein zu stärken, holte Präsident Professor Fritz Scherer die beiden anderen ehemaligen Weltklassefußballer ins Präsidium: Am 25. November 1991 wurden Beckenbauer und Rummenigge zu Vizepräsidenten gewählt. Rummenigge wurde zum »Außenminister«, auch weil er aufgrund seiner Auslandsengagements als Spieler bei Inter Mailand und Servette Genf sehr gut mehrere Fremdsprachen beherrschte. Er gründete die European Club Association (ECA) mit, deren Vorsitzender er seit 2008 auch ist. Seit 2002 ist er außerdem Vorstandsvorsitzender der FC Bayern München AG.

Beckenbauer sprang nicht nur zweimal als Trainer ein, sondern engagierte sich auch international bei FIFA, UEFA und im DFB und holte 2006 die WM als Organisationschef nach Deutschland, obwohl er von 1994 bis 2009

To understand today's FC Bayern, you need to look at the line-up in 1976. At Hampden Park in Glasgow, Bayern played in their third straight European Cup final. Their opponents were French champions AS Saint-Étienne. Bayern won their third consecutive title thanks to Franz "Bulle" Roth's winner on 57 minutes. The captain of the side was Franz Beckenbauer, at 30 years of age a global star and Bayern's undisputed leader. On offense, 24-year-old lightning-quick striker Uli Hoeneß was in his heyday. On the right side a young greenhorn played in his first final: Karl-Heinz Rummenigge got to raise the trophy at the tender age of 20.

Beckenbauer – Hoeneß – Rummenigge: three global stars, who shape Bayern to this day. It was Hoeneß, who in 1984 completed Karl-Heinz Rummenigge's transfer to Inter Milan. And Rummenigge was captain of the German side, that under team manager Franz Beckenbauer finished second in the 1986 World Cup.

The trio that defeated the French champions in 1976, later began a new career at Bayern in management. Uli Hoeneß switched sides on Mai 1, 1979, and at the age of 27 became the youngest general manager in Bundesliga history. To strengthen the level of expertise, president Fritz Scherer, Ph. D., appointed the other two former world class players to the board: on November 25, 1991, both Beckenbauer and Rummenigge were elected vice presidents. Rummenigge also became "foreign minister", since due to his stints as a player at Inter Milan and Servette Genève he was fluent in several languages. He co-founded the European Club Association (ECA), whose acting chairman he has been since 2008. Since 2002 he is also chief executive officer of the Bayern München AG.

Beckenbauer not only stepped in as interim coach on two occasions, but was involved on an international level at FIFA and UEFA as well as nationally for the DFB. From 1994 to 2009 he acted as Bayern president. And he led Germany's bid to host the 2006 World Cup and acted as chairman for the organising committee. But

gleichzeitig Präsident des FC Bayern war. Keiner aber verkörperte den FC Bayern so wie Uli Hoeneß, der mit seinen ehemaligen Mitspielern wunderbare Doppelpässe spielte. Diese geballte Fußballkompetenz der drei ehemaligen Weltklassespieler sorgt bis heute für die nationale Überlegenheit und internationale Anerkennung des Klubs.

Ja, es sind die Menschen, die einem Verein ein Gesicht geben. Ob Zufall oder nicht: Der FC Bayern hat immer wieder bayerische Galionsfiguren gefunden, die Epochen geprägt haben. Beckenbauer selbst ist in München-Giesing geboren. Gerd Müller kam mit 18 vom TSV 1861 Nördlingen, Sepp Maier mit 15 vom TSV Haar und Paul Breitner vom ESV Freilassing an der österreichischen Grenze. Klaus Augenthaler, Kapitän in den 1980ern und Anfang der 90er, stammt aus dem niederbayerischen Fürstenzell. Aus der Triple-Mannschaft 2013 wurde Kapitän Philipp Lahm in München geboren, er kam mit zwölf Jahren zum FC Bayern. Thomas Müller aus Weilheim in Oberbayern wechselte mit elf Jahren zu den Bayern. Und Bastian Schweinsteiger wurde wie Breitner in Kolbermoor geboren, gerade mal 60 Kilometer östlich von München gelegen. Seit seinem 14. Lebensjahr trug er das Bayern-Trikot, insgesamt 17 Jahre, bis er 2015 nach Manchester wechselte.

Internationale Topstars ergänzten das bayerische Gerüst zu Erfolgsteams, darunter Weltmeister wie Lizarazu und Sagnol, Strategen wie Lerby und Alonso oder Torjäger wie McInally, Makaay, Élber oder Pizarro, der erfolgreichste ausländische Torjäger der Bundesliga. Sie alle kamen beim FC Bayern zu internationaler Geltung. Um Megastars wie Messi oder Ronaldo machte der Verein allerdings stets einen großen Bogen. Denn Financial Fairplay gehört ebenfalls zu den Spielregeln der Münchner.

Zu der geballten Ladung Fachkompetenz gesellte sich schon früh der Kaufmann Karl Hopfner, der nach dem Rücktritt von Uli Hoeneß Präsident wurde, den Vorsitz im Aufsichtsrat übernahm und somit für Kontinuität sorgte.

Längst halten die Führungspersonen Ausschau nach ihren Nachfolgern. Nicht ausgeschlossen, dass ein Lahm, Müller oder Schweinsteiger irgendwann das Kompetenzteam in der Vorstandsetage ergänzen wird.

nobody shaped Bayern in the way Uli Hoeneß did, who used to play wonderful one-twos with his team mates. The concentrated footballing expertise of the three former world-class players ensures Bayern dominance on the national level to this day and won the team international recognition.

Yes, it is the people that inform a club's image. Be it by design or happy accident, FC Bayern always found Bavarian figureheads that shaped an era. Beckenbauer was born in München-Giesing. Gerd Müller came from TSV 1861 Nördlingen at age 18, Sepp Maier from TSV Haar at age 15 and Paul Breitner from ESV Freilassing near the Austrian border. Klaus Augenthaler, team captain in the 1980s and early 90s, hailed from Fürstenzell (Lower Bavaria). From the treble winning side of 2013, captain Philipp Lahm was born in Munich and joined Bayern at age 12. Thomas Müller from Weilheim in Upper Bavaria joined Bayern at age 11. And Bastian Schweinsteiger, like Breitner, was born in Kolbermoor, just 60 kilometres east of Munich. He wore the Bayern shirt since age 14, 17 years in all, before he moved to Manchester in 2015.

The Bavarian core has always been complemented by international top stars, including world champions like Lizarazu and Sagnol, strategists like Lerby or Alonso, and goal getters like McInally, Makaay, Élber and Pizarro, the most prolific foreign striker in Bundesliga history. It is players like these that brought international flair to the Bavarian club. But Bayern always steered clear of mega-stars like Messi and Ronaldo, as Financial Fair Play has always been their credo.

The concentrated football expertise was joined in 1983 by management assistant Karl Hopfner, who was appointed president after Uli Hoeneß resigned from office and also acted as chairman of the supervisory board, thus ensuring continuity.

The leaders have long since been on the lookout for their successors. It is certainly conceivable that the likes of Philipp Lahm, Thomas Müller or Bastian Schweinsteiger will one day join the expertise team on the executive floor.

»Wenn wir von der Bayern-Familie sprechen, dann betrifft das den Kreis der Mannschaft, aller Mitarbeiter und den der Fans. Der FC Bayern hat es geschafft, in die Herzen seiner Anhänger einzudringen. Das haben wir uns immer gewünscht und sind dem nun ziemlich nahegekommen.«
ULI HOENESS

"When we talk about the Bayern family, we refer to the players, the employees and the fans. The FC Bayern succeeded in gaining entry into the hearts of its supporters. This is what we have always aspired to do and what we are now close to having accomplished."
ULI HOENESS

Der FC Bayern ist mehr als nur ein Fußballklub. Er ist vor allem ein Stück bayerisches Kulturgut. Auch hinter den Kulissen werden seine professionellen Strukturen deutlich – und die gesellschaftliche Bedeutung des FC Bayern in München und darüber hinaus.

FC Bayern is much more than just a football club. It is, above all, a part of the Bavarian cultural landscape. The professional structures extend well beyond the pitch – and so does the social importance of the club in Munich and beyond.

MÜNCHEN, 25. APRIL 2009. Und manchmal wird auch um »himmlischen Beistand« gefleht. Die Nonnen aus der Kongregation der »Barmherzigen Schwestern vom hl. Vinzenz von Paul« drückten erst auf der Bank, später auf der Tribüne die Daumen für den Heimsieg gegen Schalke 04.

MUNICH, APRIL 25, 2009. It can't hurt to ask for a little divine intervention: The nuns of the congregation of the "Sisters of Charity of Saint Vincent de Paul" cross their fingers, first on the bench and later in the stands, for a home win against Schalke 04.

adidas
Home
adidas
SCHWEINSTEIGER

MÜNCHEN, 22. JULI 1995. Uli Hoeneß baute das Merchandising für den FC Bayern auf und legte auch selbst Hand an beim Verkauf. Hier steht der Manager persönlich am Tresen, rollt ein Mannschaftsposter zusammen und bietet Fanartikel im mobilen Fanshop an.

MUNICH, JULY 22, 1995. Uli Hoeneß built Bayern's merchandising department and wasn't above lending a hand in the mobile fan shop. Here the manager personally mans the counter, rolling a team poster and selling merchandise.

Jumbo-
Schal
DM 150,-
40,-
30,- DM
25,-
14,- DM
FC BAYERN M
FC BAYERN MÜNCHEN e.V.
OPEL
T-Shirt 20,-
T-Shirt 25,-

MÜNCHEN, 25. AUGUST 2014. Ein Mannschaftsfoto der etwas anderen Art. Die Bayern präsentieren sich in ihrem neuen Ausgeh-Look. Entworfen wurde die Kollektion vom italienischen Modedesigner Giorgio Armani. Robben, Neuer, Schweinsteiger, Lahm, Lewandowski, Müller, Guardiola, Boateng und Götze werden ins rechte Licht gerückt.

MUNICH, AUGUST 25, 2014. A team photo of a rather different kind. The Bayern pros showcase their new leisure wear by Italian designer Giorgio Armani. Robben, Neuer, Schweinsteiger, Lahm, Lewandowski, Müller, Guardiola, Boateng and Götze are presented in the proper light.

LEIPZIG, 19. JULI 1997. Auch Sommerregen kann ganz schön heftig werden. Beim Freundschaftsspiel in Leipzig steht sogar die Tartanbahn unter Wasser. Da muss Giovanni Trapattoni abheben, um nicht nass zu werden.

LEIPZIG, JULY 19, 1997. Even a summer rain can turn into a torrential downpour. At a friendly match in Leipzig, even the tartan track is submerged. Giovanni Trapattoni needs some elevation to stay dry.

WER

MÜNCHEN, 4. MÄRZ 1971. Bayern gegen Liverpool im März 1971: Was lag da näher, als sich mit Beatles-Musik auf das große Match im damaligen Messepokal einzustimmen? Franz Roth, Sepp Maier, Johnny Hansen und Hans-Georg Schwarzenbeck besorgten sich Perücken, bauten die Instrumente an der Säbener Straße auf und versuchten sich für den Fotografen als Doubles der legendären Liverpooler Pilzköpfe.

MUNICH, MARCH 4, 1971. When Bayern faced Liverpool in the Inter-Cities Fairs Cup in March 1971, Franz Roth, Sepp Maier, Johnny Hansen and Hans-Georg Schwarzenbeck tuned up for the game in style. They donned wigs, grabbed instruments and posed as Liverpool's legendary Fab Four.

MÜNCHEN, 3. FEBRUAR 2006. Es scheint, als brenne der Rasen. Dieser ungewöhnliche Einblick in die Tiefen der Allianz Arena wurde dem Fotografen bei der Installation von Licht, das für besseres Wachstum des Rasens sorgt, gewährt. Die eingeschalteten Lichtelemente tauchen die Arena in eine gespenstische Atmosphäre.

MUNICH, FEBRUARY 3, 2006. The pitch appears to be on fire. This unusual glimpse into the depth of the Allianz Arena was afforded during the installation of light that stimulates the growth of the grass. The engaged light elements immerse the Arena in a ghostly ambience.

MÜNCHEN, 30. JULI 1970. Als der bisherige DFB-Trainer Udo Lattek im März 1970 zum FC Bayern wechselte, holte er im Sommer als Antrittsgeschenk zwei Jugendnationalspieler nach: Uli Hoeneß aus Ulm und Paul Breitner vom ESV Freilassing. Die beiden Junggesellen, gerade 18 Jahre jung, bildeten zu Beginn eine Männer-WG und kochten sogar zusammen.

MUNICH, JULY 30, 1970. When former DFB coach Udo Lattek joined Bayern in March 1970, he brought along two players he had groomed in the German youth team: Uli Hoeneß from TSG Ulm and Paul Breitner from ESV Freilassing. The two 18-year-olds knew each other well from various matches with the national team and got along like a house on fire, so they decided to become flat mates when they moved to Munich. Household chores were evenly split: Paul took care of cooking, Uli made the beds.

BERLIN, 17. MAI 2014. Pep Guardiola im Fokus der Fotografen: Der Spanier, begehrtester Trainer der Welt, gab den Bayern noch mehr internationales Flair und führte seine Mannschaft in seinem ersten Jahr zum Double. Hier darf er den Berliner Nachthimmel genießen.

BERLIN, MAY 17, 2014. Pep Guardiola in focus: The Spaniard, the most coveted coach on the planet when he joined Bayern, brought even more international flair to Munich and led the team to a domestic double in his first season at the helm. Here he gets to enjoy the Berlin night sky.

DOUBLE
10
T . .

MÜNCHEN, 24. FEBRUAR 2004. Das Selbstbewusstsein der Bayern-Fans kennt keine Grenzen. Vor dem Spiel gegen Real Madrid zeigen sie nicht nur riesige Banner ihres Klubs, sondern schmettern auch aus vollem Herzen »Hier regiert der FCB«. Trotzdem reicht es nur zu einem 1:1, Bayern scheidet im Achtelfinale der Champions League aus.

MUNICH, FEBRUARY 24, 2004. The self-confidence of the fans knows no boundaries. Ahead of the game against Real Madrid, they not only show huge Bayern emblems but also proudly proclaim: "Hier regiert der FCB" (Here reigns FCB). Alas, the home team only managed a 1-1 draw, Bayern bowed out in the Round of 16.

24. FEB.
2004
SHARP

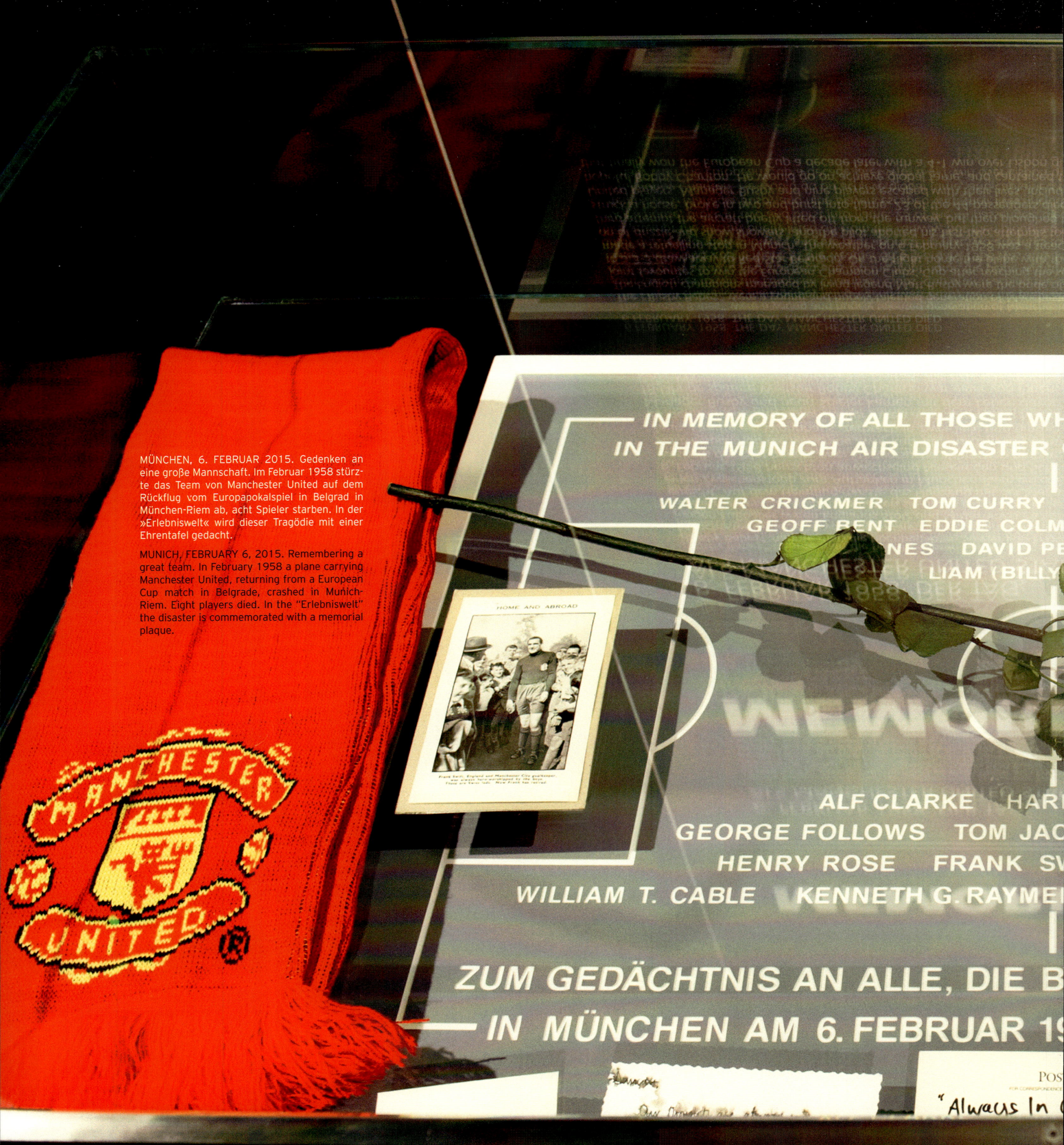

MÜNCHEN, 6. FEBRUAR 2015. Gedenken an eine große Mannschaft. Im Februar 1958 stürzte das Team von Manchester United auf dem Rückflug vom Europapokalspiel in Belgrad in München-Riem ab, acht Spieler starben. In der »Erlebniswelt« wird dieser Tragödie mit einer Ehrentafel gedacht.

MUNICH, FEBRUARY 6, 2015. Remembering a great team. In February 1958 a plane carrying Manchester United, returning from a European Cup match in Belgrade, crashed in Munich-Riem. Eight players died. In the "Erlebniswelt" the disaster is commemorated with a memorial plaque.

Das Gedenken lebt in München fort
An einer Außenwand des Old Trafford-Stadions hängt eine unauffällig gestaltete Uhr. Sie heißt „Munich Clock", und die Aufschrift „Feb 6th 1958" erinnert an den schmerzhaftesten Moment in der Vereinsgeschichte von Manchester United. Damals waren bei einer Flugzeug-Katastrophe acht Spieler der jungen Profi-Mannschaft ums Leben gekommen: Geoff Bent, Roger Byrne, Eddie Colman, Mark Jones, David Pegg, Billy Whelan, Tommy Taylor und Duncan Edwards. Auch in München wird des Unglücks regelmäßig gedacht. Der FC Bayern und besonders sein Verwaltungsbeirats-Mitglied Hermann Memmel haben dafür gesorgt, dass die Erinnerung erhalten bleibt. So wurde an der Unfallstelle im Stadtteil Kirchtrudering ein Gedenkstein errichtet. Den Ort des Crashs, Ecke Emplstraße/Rappenweg, benannte die Stadt München in Manchesterplatz um. Zum 50. Jahrestag im Jahr 2008 kam dorthin eine Delegation aus Manchester mit Bobby Charlton an der Spitze, einem der Überlebenden des Desasters. Noch heute besuchen viele Fans aus der ganzen Welt das Monument und legen Schals, Fahnen oder Briefe nieder, die vom FC Bayern Fan Club „Red Docs" eingesammelt und aufbewahrt werden. Meistens steht darin: „We will never forget you" – wir werden euch nie vergessen.
Sie sehen hier eine Replik des Gedenksteins vom Manchesterplatz in München.
Ein Ort der Erinnerung: An der Einweihung des Gedenksteins am
München im Jahr 2004 nahmen unter anderem Karl-Heinz
Alex Ferguson, Joy Worth (Witwe des damaligen Kapitäns
Memmel teil (von rechts nach links).
A place of remembrance: those present at the ceremony to
in Manchesterplatz in Munich in 2004 included (right to
Bobby Charlton, Alex Ferguson, Joy Worth (widow of the
Hermann Memmel.
The memory lives on in Munich
A simple clock hangs on a wall in
Trafford. It is named the "Munich
"Feb 6th 1958" as a memorial
Manchester United's long
youthful first team lost their
Geoff Bent, Roger Byrne,
Billy Whelan, Tommy Taylor
is also commemorated in
and in particular
ensured that the
the site of the crash
site on the corner of
Manchesterplatz
On the 50th
Sir Bobby
ceremony at the
many fans from
at the
Fan Club
"We will
The
LOST THEIR LIVES HERE
ON THE 6TH FEBRUARY 1958
ROGER BYRNE
DUNCAN EDWARDS
TOMMY TAYLOR
(DON) DAVIES
ARCHIE LEDBROKE
ERIC THOMPSON
B.P. MIKLOS
WILLIAM SATINOFF
DER FLUGZEUGKATASTROPHE
58 HIER UMS LEBEN KAMEN
30th MARCH
FOREVER IN

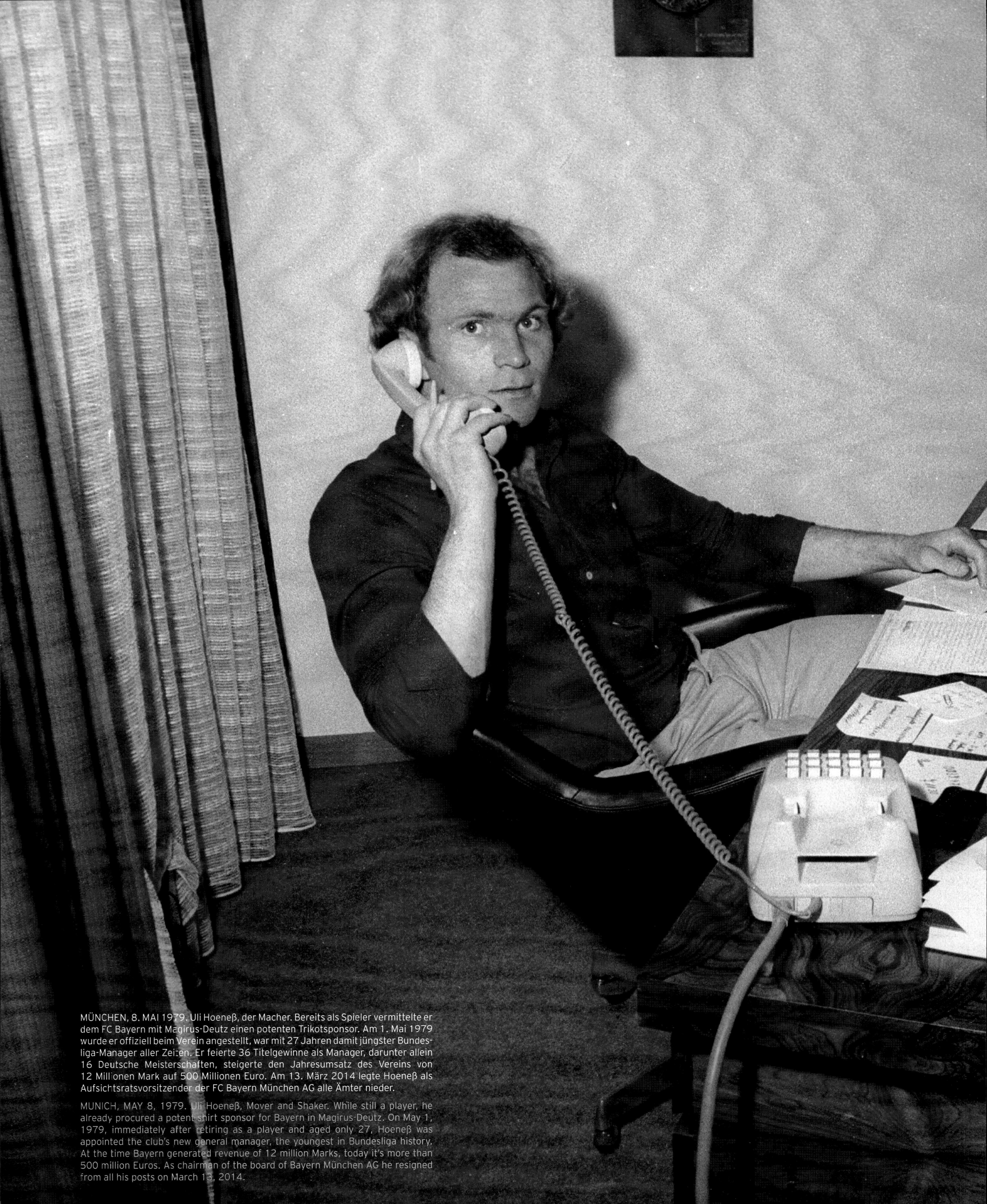

MÜNCHEN, 8. MAI 1979. Uli Hoeneß, der Macher. Bereits als Spieler vermittelte er dem FC Bayern mit Magirus-Deutz einen potenten Trikotsponsor. Am 1. Mai 1979 wurde er offiziell beim Verein angestellt, war mit 27 Jahren damit jüngster Bundesliga-Manager aller Zeiten. Er feierte 36 Titelgewinne als Manager, darunter allein 16 Deutsche Meisterschaften, steigerte den Jahresumsatz des Vereins von 12 Millionen Mark auf 500 Millionen Euro. Am 13. März 2014 legte Hoeneß als Aufsichtsratsvorsitzender der FC Bayern München AG alle Ämter nieder.

MUNICH, MAY 8, 1979. Uli Hoeneß, Mover and Shaker. While still a player, he already procured a potent shirt sponsor for Bayern in Magirus-Deutz. On May 1, 1979, immediately after retiring as a player and aged only 27, Hoeneß was appointed the club's new general manager, the youngest in Bundesliga history. At the time Bayern generated revenue of 12 million Marks, today it's more than 500 million Euros. As chairman of the board of Bayern München AG he resigned from all his posts on March 13, 2014.

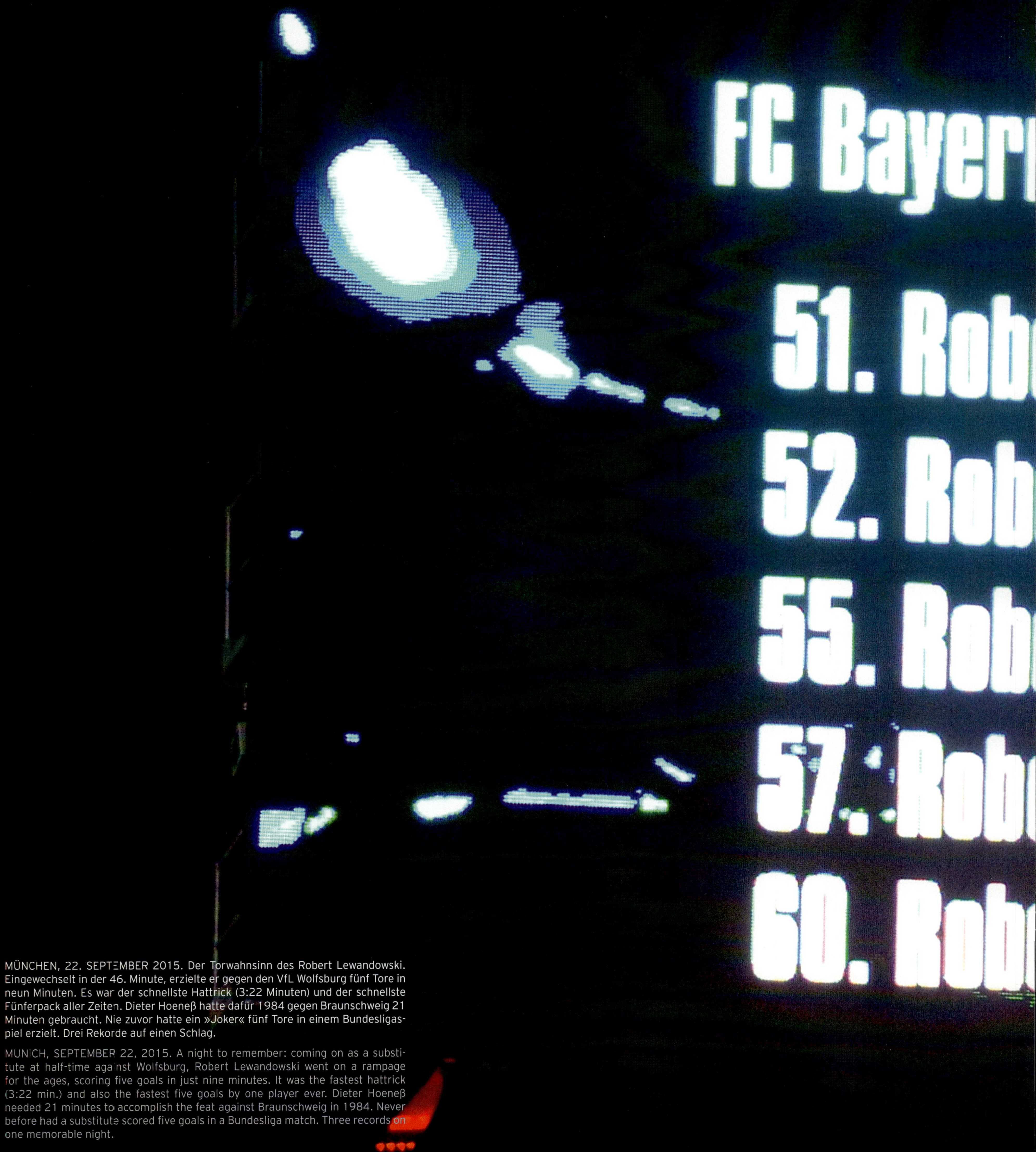

MÜNCHEN, 22. SEPTEMBER 2015. Der Torwahnsinn des Robert Lewandowski. Eingewechselt in der 46. Minute, erzielte er gegen den VfL Wolfsburg fünf Tore in neun Minuten. Es war der schnellste Hattrick (3:22 Minuten) und der schnellste Fünferpack aller Zeiten. Dieter Hoeneß hatte dafür 1984 gegen Braunschweig 21 Minuten gebraucht. Nie zuvor hatte ein »Joker« fünf Tore in einem Bundesligaspiel erzielt. Drei Rekorde auf einen Schlag.

MUNICH, SEPTEMBER 22, 2015. A night to remember: coming on as a substitute at half-time against Wolfsburg, Robert Lewandowski went on a rampage for the ages, scoring five goals in just nine minutes. It was the fastest hattrick (3:22 min.) and also the fastest five goals by one player ever. Dieter Hoeneß needed 21 minutes to accomplish the feat against Braunschweig in 1984. Never before had a substitute scored five goals in a Bundesliga match. Three records on one memorable night.

5:1 VfL Wolfsburg
ert Lewandowski
ert Lewandowski
ert Lewandowski
ert Lewandowski
ert Lewandowski

MÜNCHEN, 12. MAI 1990. Intimer Einblick in den Meistertrubel 1990. Radmilo Mihajlovic, Klaus Augenthaler und Jürgen Kohler zeigen Brust und lassen die Champagnerkorken knallen.

MUNICH, MAY 12, 1990. An intimate insight into the 1990 championship frenzy. Radmilo Mihajlovic, Klaus Augenthaler and Jürgen Kohler bare their chests and pop the champagne corks.

MÜNCHEN, 22. JUNI 1999. Giesing ist ein Münchner Arbeiterviertel. Hier, in der Zugspitzstraße 6, wuchs Franz Beckenbauer auf. Oben im vierten Stock war sein Zuhause. Und in diesem Hinterhof malträtierte er die Hauswände. Gleich gegenüber der Aschenplatz des SC 1906 München, seines Heimatvereins. 3,8 Kilometer entfernt liegt die Säbener Straße, die Heimat des FC Bayern. Dorthin wechselte er im Alter von 14 Jahren.

MUNICH, JUNE 22, 1999. Giesing is a blue-collar neighbourhood in south-eastern Munich. Here, on the fourth floor in the Zugspitzstrasse 6, is where Franz Beckenbauer grew up. And this is the backyard where young Franz used to kick balls at the walls. Across the street: the cinder pitch of his first club SC München 1906. And 3.8 km from here the Säbener Strasse, home of FC Bayern, the club he joined at the age of 14 and where he began his exceptional career.

MÜNCHEN, 4. OKTOBER 2014. Posten und twittern gehört zum modernen Kundenservice. Robert Lewandowski setzt mit einer Handy-Kamera die Fans in Szene und fotografiert sich gleich mit. Ein Selfie als Kommunikationsmittel der Neuzeit.

MUNICH, OCTOBER 4, 2014. Posting and tweeting are part of our modern way of life. Robert Lewandowski captures the fans and himself with his mobile, a selfie as a means of communication in modern times.

MÜNCHEN, 1975. Sepp Maier lachte selbst dann noch, wenn ihm der Dreck im Gesicht klebte. Er war Mister Zuverlässig, fehlte in seiner langen Karriere nur in drei Spielen während der Saison 1965/66. Seine 442 Spiele in Serie sind bis heute absoluter Bundesliga-Rekord.

MUNICH, 1975. Even with his face covered in dirt, Sepp Maier never stopped smiling. The goalkeeper was a model of consistency and missed just three matches (in the 1965-66 season) during his long career. He appeared in 442 consecutive games, a Bundesliga record to this day.

MÜNCHEN, 5. OKTOBER 2014. Das Oktoberfest ist das größte Volksfest der Welt und lockt jährlich mehr als sechs Millionen Besucher an. Es beginnt jeweils am Samstag nach dem 15. September und dauert 16 bis 18 Tage. Mittendrin in einem der 29 Festzelte ist auch der FC Bayern. Zum einen gilt »Verlieren verboten« für die Zeit des Oktoberfests, zum anderen gehört auch ein Besuch in traditioneller Tracht zu den Ritualen des Vereins. Hier bahnt sich Manuel Neuer seinen Weg.

MUNICH, OCTOBER 5, 2014. With more than six million visitors from around the globe every year, the Oktoberfest is the largest festival in the world. It begins on the first Saturday after September 15 and runs for 16 to 18 days. The Oktoberfest is an important fixture in FC Bayern's schedule: losing is strictly forbidden for the duration of the festival and a visit to one of the 29 party tents – dressed, of course, in traditional attire – is a cherished club tradition. Here, Manuel Neuer cuts a striking figure.

PARIS, 28. MAI 1975. Bayerische Fankultur im Pariser Prinzenparkstadion: Beim Europapokal-Finale 1975 durften weder Lederhosen noch Kuhglocken fehlen. Das Foto legt aber auch Zeugnis ab von der damaligen Bart- und Brillenmode.

PARIS, MAY 28, 1975. Bavarian fan culture in Paris' Parc des Princes: Bayern supporters brought Lederhosen and cow bells to the 1975 European Cup final – as well as their then fashionable beards and glasses.

HANNOVER, 18. FEBRUAR 1982. Die Piper Seneca ist ein Haufen Schrott. Bei dichtem Nebel ist das Privatflugzeug am Tag zuvor in der Nähe von Hannover abgestürzt. Die Insassen waren auf dem Weg zum Länderspiel gegen Portugal. Drei von ihnen starben. Der einzige Überlebende ist Uli Hoeneß.

HANOVER, FEBRUARY 18, 1982. Only a pile of debris remained of the Piper Seneca. The day before, the private aircraft crashed in dense fog near Hanover. Its passengers were on their way to an international match versus Portugal. Three of them perished, the sole survivor is Uli Hoeneß.

MÜNCHEN, 22. MAI 1999. Mario Basler als Entertainer. Beim 4:2 über den VfL Bochum übt sich der Mittelfeldspieler im Versteckspiel hinter »kicker«-Fotograf Herbert Liedel. Damit provoziert er das Sportfoto des Jahres 1999.

MUNICH, MAY 22, 1999. Mario Basler as a jokester and prankster. Little does he know that when he is playing hide and seek with "kicker" photographer Herbert Liedel he is staging what turns out to be the 1999 Sport Photo of the Year.

Munich, 1971. Until 1971 the dressing room was a simple wooden structure (far left in the photo). According to Franz Beckenbauer, the players would still change in that shack had Gerd Müller not scored as many goals as he did. It wasn't until later that the club offices at Säbener Strasse were established, which since then have been reconstructed and expanded numerous times.

FC. BAYERN

MÜNCHEN, APRIL 1987. Sie stehen wie eine Mauer hinter ihrer Mannschaft und sitzen manchmal auch wie die Hühner auf der Stange. Die treuen Fans sind das größte Kapital des FC Bayern. Und wer etwas auf sich hält, geht in die Südkurve. Das gehörte schon im Olympiastadion zum guten Ton.

MUNICH, APRIL, 1987. They stand like a wall behind their team and sometimes they sit like chickens on the pole. FC Bayern would be nothing without their faithful supporters. The most loyal of them gather on the South stand. It has been that way even back in the days of the Olympiastadion.

STAMMTISCH
MÜNCHBERG
F.C. BAYERN
MÜNCHEN E.V.
Südkurve
F.C. BAYERN
MÜNCHEN E.V.
FAN-BLOCK
SÜD-KURVE

MÜNCHEN, 17. MAI 2008. Der Marienplatz ist seit 1158 das historische Zentrum von München. Hier treffen Geschichte und Gegenwart aufeinander, hier tobt das Münchner Leben. Aber nie ist es hier so voll wie bei den Meisterfeiern des FC Bayern. Bis zu 100.000 Fußballfans drängeln sich dann auf dem 100 Meter langen und 50 Meter breiten Platz, um ihren Helden mit den Pokalen auf dem Rathausbalkon zuzujubeln.

MUNICH, MAY 17, 2008. The Marienplatz has been Munich's main square since 1158. For the Bavarian capital it is a confluence of past and present. The square, which is a mere 100 m long and 50 m wide, is teeming with life, but it is never as packed as for the championship celebrations of FC Bayern. Up to 100,000 fans gather here to honour their heroes, who appear with the trophies on the famous Town Hall balcony.

Deutsche Bank
AUGEN KLINIK
SWAROVSKI
GLÜCKWUNSCH!

MÜNCHEN, 16. DEZEMBER 2014. Das Flutlicht in der Allianz Arena verformt sich zu einem Stern. Und wird so zum Symbol für das Vereinslied, das den Titel »Stern des Südens« trägt. Der Titel wurde komponiert von Willy Astor, den Text schrieb Stephan Lehmann. Wenn der Refrain angestimmt wird (»FC Bayern – Stern des Südens, Du wirst niemals untergehn, weil wir in guten wie in schlechten Zeiten zueinander stehn«), singt das ganze Stadion mit.

MUNICH, DECEMBER 16, 2014. The Allianz Arena floodlights align in the shape of a star and thus the symbol of the official anthem of the club, "Stern des Südens" ("Star of the South"). It was composed by Willy Astor and texted by Stephan Lehmann. When the chorus is struck up ("FC Bayern, Star of the South, you will never go down, because we will stand together in good and in bad times"), the whole stadium erupts.

MÜNCHEN, 10. MAI 2014. Einst war München die Stadt der Biere. Heute gibt es hier immerhin noch sechs große Bierkonzerne. Und das Hofbräuhaus gehört ebenso zur bayerischen Metropole wie die Biergärten. Beim FC Bayern hat die Bierdusche Tradition, Titel werden mit dem klebrigen Nass aus überdimensionalen Weißbiergläsern gefeiert. Da gibt es kein Entrinnen, für keinen Spieler und keinen Trainer, wie hier Pep Guardiola durch Daniel van Buyten erfahren muss.

MUNICH, MAY 10, 2014. Munich used to be the city of beers. Today there are still six major breweries left. And the Hofbräuhaus is as much a part of the Bavarian metropolis as a myriad of beer gardens. At FC Bayern, the beer shower is a treasured tradition and championships are celebrated with the golden liquid from oversized Weissbier glasses. There's no escaping, not for the players and not for the coaches either, as Pep Guardiola learns here at the hands of Daniel van Buyten.

PAULANER
BAYERN MÜNCHEN
5

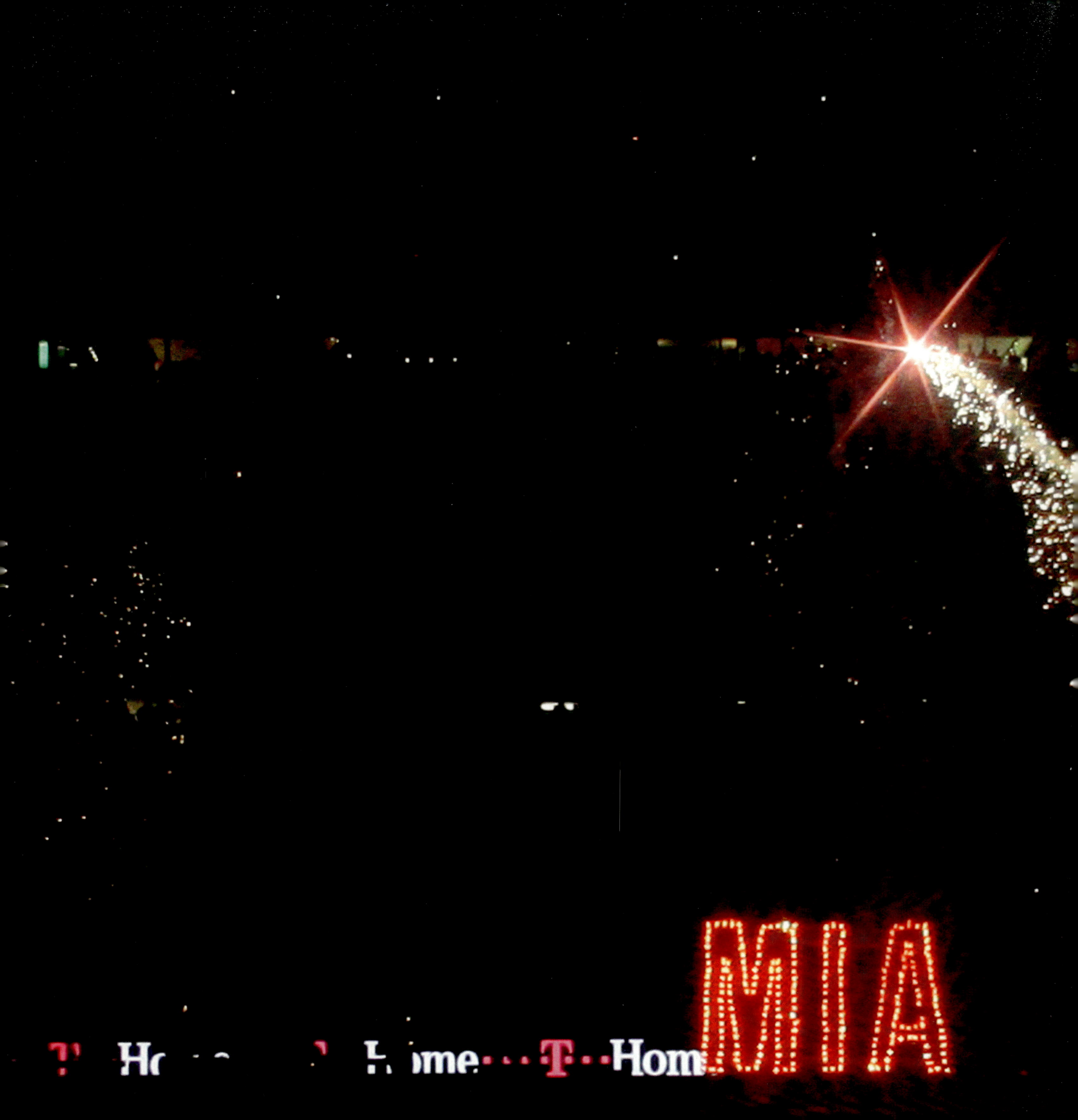

MÜNCHEN, 27. FEBRUAR 2010. Den Slogan »Mia san Mia« hat der FC Bayern adaptiert. Er stammt aus den Zeiten der KuK-Dynastie und heißt in bayerischem Dialekt »Wir sind wir«. Seine symbolische Bedeutung: eine Bekundung von Selbstbewusstsein und gleichzeitig ein Ausdruck von Bodenständigkeit und Tradition. Werte, die beim FC Bayern großgeschrieben werden.

MUNICH, FEBRUARY 27, 2010. FC Bayern adopted the catchphrase "mia san mia" as their official slogan in 2012. It dates back to the Austro-Hungarian Empire and means, in Bavarian dialect, "us are us". Its symbolic meaning: to be an expression of confidence combined with down-to-earthness and tradition. Values which are a big part of Bayern's identity.

SAN MIA

FC BAYERN IST EIN STÜCK MÜNCHNER KULTUR

FC BAYERN – A PIECE OF BAVARIA'S CULTURAL HERITAGE

Die Bayern sind anders. Sie tragen Tracht, sie essen Weißwürste, sie blasen in Alphörner. Bayern, mit 70.000 Quadratkilometern das flächenmäßig größte deutsche Bundesland, ist seit 1918 ein Freistaat. Es zählt 12,7 Millionen Einwohner und würde als eigenständiger Staat zu den zehn größten in Europa zählen.

Bei einer Umfrage darüber, was die besondere bayerische Lebensart bedeutet, wurde im Jahr 2009 neben Tracht, Oktoberfest, Brauchtum, Bier, Landschaft, Bergen und Schlössern der FC Bayern genannt. Denn der Klub ist auch ein Stück Münchner Kultur. Und diese Kultur wird gepflegt.

Jeder Trainer, jeder neue Spieler erhält quasi mit der Vertragsunterschrift eine maßgeschneiderte Lederhose. So reagierte der ehemalige Präsident Willi O. Hoffmann auf die Fangesänge in fremden Stadien, die oftmals »Zieht den Bayern die Lederhosen aus« intonierten. Demonstrativ stellten die Bayern die Lederhosen zur Schau und dokumentierten so bayerisches Selbstbewusstsein. Ein jährlicher Besuch auf dem Oktoberfest, dem bekanntesten Volksfest der Welt, ist ebenso obligatorisch wie die Erfüllung der Vorgabe, binnen dieser zwei Wochen kein Spiel zu verlieren (was meistens gelingt).

Auch der Bierdusche, die traditionell jede Titelfeier begleitet, kann sich kein Spieler und kein Trainer entziehen. Und zu jeder Titelfeier gehört eine neue Choreografie. Da werden dann auch schon mal besagte Alphörner geblasen. Der FC Bayern pflegt dieses Brauchtum.

Dazu ist der Verein in allen gesellschaftlichen Bereichen präsent. Spieler wurden zu Schauspielern – wie Paul Breitner in dem Western »Potato Fritz«. Sie werden zu begehrten Werbeträgern wie Franz Beckenbauer. Seine Reklame für einen Suppenhersteller (»Kraft in den Teller, Knorr auf den Tisch«) ist ebenso legendär wie diejenige für eine Telefongesellschaft (»Ja ist denn heut' scho' Weihnachten?«).

Bavarians are different. They wear "Trachten", they eat "Weißwürstl", they blow "Alphörner". Bavaria, Germany's largest state with an area of 70,000 square kilometres, has been a free state since 1918. With 12.7 million inhabitants, Bavaria as an independent state would be among the ten largest in Europe.

In a 2009 survey asking what is unique about the Bavarian way of life, FC Bayern was one of the top responses, along with Tracht, Oktoberfest, tradition, beer, scenery, mountains and castles. For FC Bayern is a part of Munich's cultural heritage – and this heritage is cultivated.

Every new player and every new coach receives a custom-made lederhosen virtually by signing the contract. That's how former president Willi O. Hoffmann responded to the often-heard chants in opposing stadiums, where fans intoned "Zieht den Bayern die Lederhosen aus" ("Take off their lederhosen"). So Bayern pointedly donned lederhosen, displaying their unbridled confidence. An annual visit to the Oktoberfest, the biggest festival in the world, is now as much a part of Bayern tradition as is their aspiration not to lose in the two weeks the festival is running (which they usually succeed in).

Another custom that players and coaches gladly partake in is the beer shower, an integral and delightful aspect of every championship party, as are alphorns and whipcracking. FC Bayern fosters and cherishes these traditions.

Bayern is well represented in all walks of life. Some of their players became actors, like Paul Breitner, who starred in the western "Potato Fritz". They are in demand as celebrities for advertising, like Franz Beckenbauer. His commercials for packet soup ("Power in the plate, Knorr on the table") and a telecommunications operator ("Well, is it Christmas already?") were instant

Sie haben sich als Sänger versucht wie Beckenbauer mit »Gute Freunde kann niemand trennen«. Auch wenn der Erfolg in den deutschen Hitparaden bescheiden ausfiel, so half dieser Titel 1967 immerhin der Fernsehlotterie. Denn Bayern stellt seine Popularität auch in den Dienst sozialer Einrichtungen, übernimmt so auch gesellschaftliche Verantwortung. Und Bayern-Spieler werden zu begehrten TV-Experten. Die Münchner Ex-Profis Mehmet Scholl (ARD) und Oliver Kahn (ZDF) kommentieren öffentlich-rechtlich, Franz Beckenbauer wurde zum Aushängeschild des Pay-TV-Senders Sky.

Bei Madame Tussauds im Berliner Wachsfigurenkabinett schließlich ist seit kurzer Zeit neben Franz Beckenbauer und Oliver Kahn auch Manuel Neuer ausgestellt, der beste Torhüter der WM 2014.

Der FC Bayern hat den Anspruch, in allen Belangen eine echte Nummer eins zu sein. Dazu gehört auch das vereinseigene Gelände an der Säbener Straße mitten in München, das Service-Center, Leistungszentrum, Trainingsplätze, Verwaltungsgebäude sowie ein Jugendhaus umfasst und kontinuierlich erweitert und umgebaut wird. Schmuckstück ist die ebenfalls vereinseigene Allianz Arena, die zur Weltmeisterschaft 2006 im Münchner Norden neu erbaut wurde. Die Verpflichtungen aus der Finanzierung sind seit 2014 getilgt und damit 14 Jahre vor dem errechneten Zeitpunkt. Möglich wurde das durch den Einstieg des Versicherungskonzerns und Stadion-Namensgebers in die FC Bayern München AG. Jeweils 8,33 Prozent halten auch der Sportartikelhersteller adidas und der Autobauer Audi, die so ihre weltweite Präsenz mit der des FC Bayern verbinden und durch das Engagement die Verbindung zu dem Klub zementiert haben.

Ein Blick auf den Aufsichtsrat zeigt auch die Vernetzung mit Politik und Wirtschaft. Mit Professor Rupert Stadler (Audi), Timotheus Höttges (Telekom) und Herbert Hainer (adidas) engagieren sich drei Vorstandsvorsitzende von großen deutschen Unternehmen in diesem Kontrollgremium, zu dem auch Dr. Edmund Stoiber gehört, der ehemalige bayerische Ministerpräsident.

Man sieht also: Der FC Bayern hält auch national Verbindung zu Vertretern aller Gesellschaftsschichten.

classics. The Kaiser also tried his hand at singing with the song "Gute Freunde kann niemand trennen" ("Good friends cannot be separated"). Not much of a chart hit, mind you, but it certainly helped along a TV lottery that raises funds for charitable causes. Bayern often lent their popularity for the greater good, supporting social service providers thus assuming social responsibility.

Bayern players are in high demand as TV pundits. Both German public broadcasting services employ former FCB stars – ARD with Mehmet Scholl and ZDF with Oliver Kahn. Franz Beckenbauer meanwhile remains a figurehead for pay TV channel Sky.

Beckenbauer and Kahn are also featured at Madame Tussauds wax museum in Berlin. Recently they got company in Manuel Neuer, the best goalkeeper at the 2014 World Cup.

FC Bayern aspires to be a true number one in all areas. An important aspect of this endeavour are the club-owned training facilities at Säbener Strasse in the heart of Munich, which are constantly expanded. So far, they include a service centre, a performance centre, training grounds, offices as well as a youth academy. Cream of the crop is the Allianz Arena, also owned by the club, which was constructed prior to the World Cup 2006 in the North of Munich. The financing has been completed in 2014, 14 years ahead of the target date, made possible by the involvement of the insurance company that also owns the stadium's naming rights. Allianz now holds an 8.33% stake of Bayern München, as do sporting goods manufacturer adidas and automobile manufacturer Audi, who both tie their worldwide commitments to FC Bayern, thus cementing the relationship.

A glance at the board of directors reveals the connection to politics and economy. In Rupert Stadler, Ph.D. (Audi), Timotheus Höttges (Telekom) and Herbert Hainer (adidas), three top CEOs of big German companies are involved in the supervisory committee that also features former Bavarian minister-president Edmund Stoiber.

This, too, is proof of the strong bond FC Bayern maintains to all social classes.

DER AUTOR

Ulrich Kühne-Hellmessen (Jhrg. 1957) hat als Autor, Herausgeber und Produzent über 60 Sportbücher veröffentlicht. Darunter Bestseller wie »*Verrückter Fußball*«, »*Lothar Matthäus, mein Tagebuch*« oder »*Der Triumph von Rio*« über die Fußball-WM 2014. Zuvor war der Österreicher in leitenden Positionen für das *Westfalen-Blatt/Bielefeld* und das *kicker*-Sportmagazin, *Sport-Bild*, *Bild*, *Blick* in Zürich und die *dapd* in Berlin tätig. Als Geschäftsführer leitete er den *Sportverlag Europa*, die *Cosmo Beratungs AG* und die Agentur *KBsports*. Über den FC Bayern veröffentlichte er unter anderem die Werke »*Triple 2013*« und »*Die 25. Meisterschaft*« 2015.

FOTONACHWEISE

FC Bayern
Seite 1, 24, 38, 184, 186, 240

Andreas Blumenthal
Seite 226

Bernd Ducke
Seite 34

Getty Images
Seite 2, 4, 14, 20, 22, 26, 30, 32, 36, 46, 50, 62, 66, 80, 84, 86, 88, 94, 96, 98, 102, 104, 106, 108, 122, 124, 128, 130, 132, 136, 148, 162, 168, 178, 182, 188, 216, 218, 222, 228, 244, 246

Horstmüller
Seite 190

Imago
Seite 6, 56, 58, 100, 152, 154, 160, 176, 192, 214, 220, 232, 238, 242, 248

Fred Joch
Seite 8, 42, 54, 60, 68, 72, 82, 86, 112, 114, 116, 118, 120, 134, 142, 170, 174, 208, 212, 230

Christian Kaufmann
Seite 10, 28, 166, 172, 204, 210

THE AUTHOR

Ulrich Kühne-Hellmessen (b. 1957) has published more than 60 sports books as author, editor and producer, including bestselling titles like "*Verrückter Fußball*", "*Lothar Matthäus, mein Tagebuch*", and "*Der Triumph von Rio*" about the 2014 World Cup. The Austrian previously worked in leading positions for the *Westfalen-Blatt/Bielefeld*, sports magazines *kicker* and *Sport-Bild* as well as *Bild*, *Blick* in Zurich and *dapd* in Berlin. He acted as chief executive for *Sportverlag Europa*, *Cosmo Beratungs AG* and *KBsports* agency. On FC Bayern he published, among others, the titles "*Triple 2013*" and in 2015 "*Die 25. Meisterschaft*".

PHOTO CREDITS

Picture alliance
Seite 16, 70, 146, 150, 164, 180, 202, 234, 236

Hans Rauchensteiner
Seite 48, 52, 110, 126, 194, 200, 206, 224, 250

Sven Simon
Seite 76, 158

Agentur Sündhofer
Seite 18

Marco Tedeskino (für die **BILD-Zeitung**)
Seite 144

Ullstein-Bild
Seite 12, 64, 74, 78

Barbara Volkmer
Seite 254

Werek
Seite 156